BHĀVANĀKRAMA

BHĀVANĀKRAMA OF KAMALAŚILA

Translated into English
by PARMANANDA SHARMA
with a Foreword
by HIS HOLINESS THE DALAI LAMA

ADITYA PRAKASHAN
New Delhi

First published, 1997
Reprint, 2004

ISBN 81-86471-15-4

Published by P.K. Goel for Aditya Prakashan, F-14/65, Model Town II, Delhi – 110 009 and printed at Rajkamal Electric Press, Delhi – 110 033.

THE DALAI LAMA

FOREWORD

Tibetans will always remain grateful to such great Indian scholars and adepts as Shantarakshita, Padmasambhava and Dipamkara Shrijnana, who brought the Buddha's teachings to the Land of Snows. Despite the difficulties they faced, they spent the best part of their lives propagating and explaining the teachings of Sutra and Tantra for the welfare of all sentient beings. Kings, ministers, scholars and a whole class of translators worked unceasingly to render Sanskrit texts and their commentaries into Tibetan.

Acharya Kamalashila (9th century CE), a disciple of Shantarakshita, was the first Indian scholar to live and compose his writings in Tibet. Bhavana-krama (Stages of Meditation) is one such work. It comprises three parts which were probably written at different times. The focus of Bhavana-krama is the cultivation of meditative concentration and special insight. It details the sequence of meditational practices essential for understanding the true nature of phenomena.

While Tibetan and Sanskrit editions of Bhavana-krama have been in existence for centuries, no English translation of this remarkable classic was readily available. Therefore, in response to my own suggestion, Professor P.N. Sharma has undertaken the task of translating it into English. I am confident that whether they have an academic and historical view of the transmission of Buddhism to Tibet or a wish to put these teachings into actual practice, English readers will find this translation of great value.

November 5, 1996

ACKNOWLEDGEMENTS

My profoundest gratitude is due to His Holiness the Dalai Lama for assigning the work of translation to me and for gifting a copy of BHĀVANĀ-KRAMA from his personal library. Thanks are also due to my friend, Gyatsho Tshering, Director, Library of Tibetan Works and Archives, Dharamsala, for making available to me library facilities including xeroxing of the MS and to the staff of LTWA for their assistance and cooperation.

Thanks are also due to Mr. Pradeep Goel, Aditya Prakashan, publisher of this book.

Author

CONTENTS

TRANSLATOR'S NOTE

Kamalaśila is one of those distinguished āchāryas who went to Tibet from India, stayed there and wrote scholarly treatises on Buddha dharma. His historic debate with and victory over the Chinese monk, Hoshang, is considered as a landmark in the annals of the spread of Buddhism in Bod. 'Bhāvanā-krama' is one of his more important writings and comprises three chapters. Fortified with extensive quotes from innumerable sūtras, it delineates the 'krama' or sequence of meditational practice a seeker should undertake in order to attain 'sarvajñatā', the true knowledge of things. Whereas the first and the third chapters had for long been extant in Sanskrit, the second chapter was available in Tibetan version alone. It was left to Prof. Gyaltsen Namdol of the Central Institute of Higher Tibetan Studies, Varanasi to render the second chapter back into Sanskrit from Tibetan. The Institute brought out the complete version along with the Tibetan and Hindi translations. The present work is the first-ever English rendering from original Sanskrit done at the suggestion of His Holiness the Dalai Lama, the great Compassionate One, to whose gracious and constant blessings I can never adequately match my humble gratitude.

Dharamsala — Parmananda Sharma

INTRODUCTION

Padmasambhava, Śāntarakśita, Dipankara Śrijñāna and Kamalaśila together make the foursome of the great masters who made the Dharma what it came to be in Tibet. To Śāntarakśita and Kamalaśila — the teacher-pupil duo — goes the credit of propagating, preaching and developing Buddhism in Bod in all its varied nuances, thus lending it purity, originality and authenticity.

Kamalaśila wrote his 'Bhāvanākrama' in Tibet itself, keeping in view the special requirements of his Tibetan audience. Hence, his style here is that of a lucid prose-writer who deliberately clothed his lofty and abstract theme in simple, intelligible Sanskrit which is quite different from his diction in other works.

'Bhāvanākrama' is the first-ever Sanskrit text written by any Indian āchārya on the soil of Tibet. With the passage of time, copies of Bhāvanā-krama manuscripts dwindled in the monastic libraries of the country as the study of Sanskrit declined. The second chapter in original totally disappeared and whatever manuscripts remained became truncated. Of course, the Tibetan version continued to be extant in its entirety. Prof. Tucci retrieved Chapter I from Tibet and Chapter III from Russia in original Sanskrit and he published the two in Roman script.

Not much, by way of biographical information on Kamalaśila, is on record. He appears to have visited Tibet during the reign of Trison-De-tsen, the 37th King (742-798 A.D.), who invited, among others, Āchārya Śāntarakśita of Nalanda and later Padmasambhava from Urgyan to Tibet. The latter succeeded where the former had failed; the Tibetans took readily to the teachings and practices of the 'mahāsiddha' rather than to the intellectual scholasticism of Śāntarakśita who went back to India only to return later and leave his mortal coil on the soil of Tibet after many years of missionary work. Before Śāntarakśita died, he had predicted, it is said, that a time would come when the Indian and

Chinese schools would come into sharp conflict on the concepts of gradual and instant enlightenment as respectively advocated by the two sides. So he had instructed that when the exigency arose Kamalaśila, his able pupil from Nālandā, should be invited to defend the Indian point of view about the interpretation of Sūtra. A religious debate was arranged between āCharya Kamalaśila and Hoshang, the Chinese monk. It was held at Samye and covered a period of two years (792-794 A.D.). The Chinese Hoshang was defeated and the king, himself a great scholar, declared Kamalaśila the victor. To mark the great Indian āchārya's triumph, a royal proclamation was also issued in letters of gold inscribed on blue paper. This document was ordered to be preserved as a court document. The main features of the proclamation were as historic as the occasion that had led to it; the Three Gems ('tri-ratna') to be never abandoned; monasteries to be maintained and supported; all succeeding kings and members of royalty to uphold the Proclamation. Ministers and princes and army commanders took oaths of loyalty to the document of which thirteen copies were made for record. Feasting, singing and dancing festivities followed in which the royal family, including the king, cabinet members and other high dignitaries participated. The king even composed a poem to mark the occasion:-

With great toil have I gathered the treasure
and I am happy to spend without measure
in spreading the faith of the Buddha,
gleaned from the land of India,

It was in Tho-tho-ri Nyantsen's reign
that The Secret first here came;
translated in Songtsen Gampo's time,
it has become established in mine.

It is said that the Chinese circles felt extremely piqued over their defeat; it was a total loss of face for them. They were not the ones to take their defeat sportingly; their hired assasins murdered the āchārya in cold blood. The great teacher's tragic death broke the king's heart who too passed away soon after.

BHĀVANĀKRAMA - I

I shall briefly describe 'bhāvanākrama'[1] or the sequence of meditation in accordance with the rules of conduct prescribed for an 'ādikarmika'[2] in the Mahāyāna Sūtras.

Those desirous of attaining 'sarvajñatā'[3] speedily should, in essence, try to practise these three things: 'karuṇā',[4] 'bodhichitta'[5] and 'pratipatti'.[6]

Knowing that 'karuṇā' is the basic root of all dharma practices of Lord Buddha's teachings, it should be contemplated or meditated upon at the very outset. As has been said in Ārya-dharma-sangeeti: "So the bodhisattva mahāsattva Ārya Avalokiteśvara said this to Lord Buddha, 'O Lord! a bodhisattva should not receive instruction in various dharmas. If he thoroughly practises a single dharma with devotion, all other dharmas will be his. Now, what is that single dharma? It is 'mahā-karuṇā'. Through 'mahā-karuṇā' all other Buddha dharmas[7] are in the palm of a bodhisattva's hand, O Lord! just as where-so-ever a 'chakravartin' ruler's chakra-jewel moves, there do his mighty armies, so also, O Lord! where-so-ever a bodhisattva's 'mahākaruṇā' goes, thither do all Buddha dharmas follow. O Lord! just as all other senses function so long as life-breath stays so also as long as mahākaruṇā stays all other dharmas for the bodhisattvas are generated'."

It has been said in Āryākśya-mati-nirdeśa: "moreover, O bhadanta,[8] Shāradavati's son! the bodhisattvas' 'māhakaruṇā' is inexhaustible. And, how is it so? Because, it is 'purvangamā',[9] O bhadanta Shāradavati's son! just as breathing in and breathing out is the 'purvagāmi'[10] or precursor of life-breath, so also in Māhayāna, a bodhisattva's 'māhakaruṇā' is a pre-requisite for the collection of 'punya' or merit". Also, in the Ārya-gayā-śirṣa: "O Manjuśri! What is the beginning of the conduct of bodhisattvas and what their adhiṣthāna ?[11]" "Manjuśri replied 'O Deva-putra! the beginning of a bodhisattva's conduct is 'māhākaruṇā' and its adhiṣthāna the beings."

By it, i.e. 'mahākaruṇā', inspired the bodhisattvas, with

little concern for themselves, work assiduously for collecting merit through long, arduous periods of time with the sole object of others' well-being. So it has been said in Ārya-śraddhābalādhāna: "For the well-being of sattvas through 'mahākaruṇā', there is no joy which a bodhisattva does not renounce." In this manner, by engaging himself in the most difficult situations and by collecting (sambhāra)[12] merit quickly, he attains 'sarvajñatā'. Therefore, the root of all Buddha-dharmas is 'mahākaruṇā'." It was through holding on to 'mahākaruṇā' that Lord Buddha, after attaining 'sarvajñatā', continued to work for the whole world. The Lord's 'mahākaruṇā' is thus the very reason for the Lord not entering 'nirvāṇa'.

It, i.e. 'mahākaruṇā', is (born from and) augmented by constantly reflecting in the mind over the sufferings of beings. All 'sattvas' are suffering from the three-fold pain[13] of dukhas rampant in the three worlds',[14] — (reflecting) like this one should fix one's thought on all beings. The Lord has described how hell-beings continue to suffer for long periods from such tortures as fire-burning; so also 'pretas',[15] through suffering from dukha-fire with extreme hunger and thirst, get emaciated in body and suffer terribly for a hundred years even; such as these have not had even spittal to lick at. Thus has, stated the Lord. Beings born even as 'tiryakas'[16] are seen to experience great suffering through mutual anger, killings, beatings and torturing etc. For example, some have their bodies made helpless through piercing of ears, beatings and lashing and they are made to suffer by all and sundry. Their bodies get exhausted and fatigued by their having to carry loads unwillingly. Some, living in the forest, may also be searched out and killed even though they may be innocent. Some, out of mutual fear, are constantly running about here and there with minds disturbed.

Their sufferings too seem to be endless. Hell-tortures can be witnessed even during human existence, because here also things like the amputation of a thief's limbs, consignment to the scaffold and the tying down of hands and feet etc. are nothing but hell-tortures. Those who suffer from penury are experiencing the dukhas of hunger and thirst like 'pretas'. Those who as servants have subordinated their thoughts to others and those who are tortured after being over-powered by the powerful suffer from the tortures of beating and tying like 'tiraykas'. So also are immeasureable the dukhas of beings during journeys and from mutual deceit and beatings, and from union with and separation from the unloved and the loved ones respectively. The affluent ones who are considered to be happy are also liable to lose their property submerged as they are in the midst of extremely evil eyes, and owing to the accumulation of many 'kleśas' and 'karmas' which are causal to the experiencing of hell-tortures, they are like trees on the edge of a waterfall and are, in the ultimate sense, unhappy being in the midst of the causes of dukha.

Even gods do not have mental composure[17] so long as they wander in the realm of 'kāma' or desire because their minds, aflame with the raging fire of desires, are unclean and mad. What happiness can be there for these so poor in the joys of the wealth of tranquillity ?[18] What happiness can be there for them, i.e. gods, who are overcome by the constant fear of a fall (from their god-state) ? Those who, for some period (of their existence) move about in visible and invisible states (that is, with form and without form) also, though free for a while from the tortures of suffering, ultimately suffer from the dukha of evil consequences leading to hell-tortures owing to their not having overcome the 'anuśayas'[19] from a 'kāmāvachāra'[20] conduct. Thus all human beings and gods owing to their subordination to 'karma kleśas',[21] are suffering from the dukha of 'samskāra-dukha'.[22]

In this way the whole world is wrapped around by a wreath of dukha-fire; so seeing and thinking 'just as I do not like suffering so also don't others', one should generate a feeling of compassion for all beings. First of all such 'bhāvanā' or contemplation should be cultivated towards friends, keeping in mind the aforesaid experiences of dukha or suffering.

Then, with a mind introvert and staid, one should contemplate like this: 'there is not a single 'sattva' in this beginning-less world who has not been related to me a hundred times'; in this manner contemplate on ordinary beings. When compassion similar to that for one's friends is also generated for common beings, one should through 'chitta-samatā'[23] or mental equality contemplate on one's enemies also. When one is as much concerned[24] for one's enemies as for one's friends one should generate identical 'bhāvanā' or feeling for all the beings in all the ten directions one after the other. When the spontaneous desire to remove the dukha of all the sattvas like one would that of one's own dear child is generated, it (i.e. the desire) becomes 'niṣpanna'[25] or staid and is designated as 'mahākaruṇa' as has been described in Akśayamati-sūtra. This sequence of 'kripā' bhāvanā or the contemplation of compassion has been described by the Lord in the Abhidharma sūtras etc.

Through the force of the practising of such compassion and the vow of uplifting all 'sattvas', bodhichitta[26] is spontaneously born as importunate[27] for 'annuttar-samyaka-sambodhi'.[28]

As has been said in Ārya Daśa-dharma-sūtra: "Seeing that the beings are unprotected, unsheltered and homeless one should fix one's mind in 'karuṇā' so that 'anuttara samyaka-sambodhi' is generated." Even though 'bodhichitta is generated in a bodhisattva through another's adherence to 'samyaka'[29] still bodhichitta generated in a bodhisattva through the on-rush of compassion is far superior as stated in Ārya-Tāthāgata-jñāna-mudrā. Samādhi by the Lord. He (the Lord) has said that such bodhichitta is highly beneficial in the world even without 'pratipatti'.[30] As has been mentioned in Maitreya-Vimokśa: "O kulputra! just as a broken 'Vajra-ratna'[31] superimposes itself on the best of gold ornaments but still retains its identity and removes all want, similarly, O kulputra! the 'Vajra-ratna' of the generation of mind for the attainment of 'sarvajñatā',[32] even if not accompanied by 'pratipatti', superimposes itself on the gold ornaments of the 'guṇas'[33] of a 'śrāvaka'[34] and a 'pratyeka-buddha';[35] it does not abandon 'bodhichitta' and also removes the wants of the world."

He who cannot be fully and in every manner educated in the 'pāramitās'[36] should also cultivate bodhichitta, because by holding on to 'upāyaya',[37] great benefits accrue. As has been said in Ārya-rajāvavādaka-sūtra: "O king! as you are a great doer and can do a lot, it is not possible to educate everyone in every way from 'dāna-pāramitā'[38] to 'prajñā-pāramitā'[39] so you should constantly re-capitulate', mentally visualise and contemplate on your desire for and faith in prayer and determination or vow[40] for 'samyaka sambodhi' while walking, stopping, sitting, sleeping, waking, eating, drinking, recollecting all the 'kūśala-mūlas'[41] or root-merits of the Buddhas, bodhisattvas, pratyeka-buddhas, ārya-śrāvakas, common people, your own of the past, of the present, of the future, and commend them (i.e. kuśala mūlas). After 'anumodana'[42] or commending, offer it again to the Buddhas, bodhisattvas, pratyeka-buddhas, ārya-śrāvakas through worship and, after offering, make them common[43] for the common people. Then transform into 'anuttara-samyaka-sambodhi' all 'kuśalas' or merits practised thrice everyday for the attainment of 'sarvajñatā' by sattvas and for the fulfilment of all Buddha-dharmas.[44] Thus will you, O King! having become 'pratipanna' or realised, rule (your kingdom). You will not have to abandon governance and you will also accomplish 'bodhi-sambhāra'[45] or accumulation of bodhi." He further added: "as the fruit[46] of your root-merits of 'samyaka-sambodhi', many times you were born among gods, many times among men and during all your godly and human births you will be a ruler." Thus said in detail.

Bodhichitta, which is the essence of 'pratipatti' or attainment, has been proved to be immensely fruitful. As has been said in Ārya-veerdatta-pariprichhā: "If the 'punya' which is attained from bodhichitta is handsome, it will fill the entire 'ākāśa-dhātu'[47] and overflow it." "A person offers as many 'buddha-kśetras'[48] full of gems as the sands of the

Ganga to the Lords, another with folded hands bows his mind (asking) for bodhi; the latter worship is superior because it has no end." says Ārya-gandavyūha: "O Kulputra! bodhichitta is the seed of all Buddha-dharmas". This in detail. "That bodhichitta is of two kinds, 'praṇidhi'-chitta'[49] and 'prasthāna-chitta',[50] that is, the mind that is fixed on the goal and the mind that is actually treading the road to bodhi. O Kulaputre! such beings are rare in the world who fix their mind in 'anuttara-samyaka-sambodhi'; rarer even are beings who have ventured on the path of 'anuttara-samyaka-sambodhi'. May I become a Buddha for the well-being of the whole world; — such a preliminary prayer by the practitioner is called 'praṇidhi-chitta' or fixing of the mind from the moment one holds the vow ('samvara')[51] and enters 'sambhāra'[52] or accumulation (of bodhi), it is termed as 'prasthāna-chitta' or the journeying mind.

'Samvara' has to be received from other powerful and learned and 'samvara'-attuned kalyāṇ-mitras.[53] In the absence of a favourable 'grāhaka' or recepient (or giver?), bodhichitta should be generated by visualizing the Buddhas and the bodhisattvas as did Ārya Manjuśri by becoming Ambara-rāja.[54] A bodhisattva who has so generated bodhichitta himself practises 'dāna' etc. by giving and engages in 'pratipatti' knowing that if one does not oneself give away one cannot (exercise) control (over) others. And, there is no attainment of bodhi without 'pratipatti' or the knowledge of the eight-fold path.

As has been said in Ārya-gayāśirṣa, "The bodhisattvas with 'pratipatti' achieve bodhi and not those without "pratipatti". It has also been stated in Ārya-samādhi-rāja: "O Kumāra! you should thus-wise instruct yourself: 'I shall possess the essence of 'pratipatti.' What for thus ? Because, O Kumāra! for one possessing the essence of 'pratipatti', 'anuttara-samyaka-sambodhi' is not difficult to attain."

The 'pratipatti' of the bodhisattva along with the differentiation of 'pāramitā', 'apramāṇa'[55] and 'samgraha-vastu'[56] etc. has been described in detail in sūtras like

Akśyamati-ratnamegha-sūtra. When a bodhisattva has to learn even such material subjects as 'śilpa',[57] what then to speak of transcendental dhyāna etc.? Otherwise, how will he fulfil all his commitments towards sattvas? Hence, in brief, the 'prajñā' and 'upāyaya'[58] of a bodhisattva are neither only 'prajñā' nor only 'upāyaya' alone. As has been said in Ārya Vimala-kīrti-nirdeśa: "'prajñā' without 'upāyaya' and 'upāyaya' without 'prajñā' are a bondage for the bodhisattva." 'Upāyaya' (means) with 'prajñā' (wisdom) and 'prajñā' with 'upāyaya' are described as release. It is also said in Ārya-gayāśirṣa: "In brief, these are the two paths for a bodhisattva. Equipped with this twin path, the 'mahā-sattva' bodhisattva will soon be linked with 'anuttara-samyaka-sambodhi' or supreme enlightenment. What are these two? These are 'upāyaya' and 'prajñā'.

Here, leaving aside the Perfection of Wisdom, all others such as the perfection of 'dāna', 'samgrah-vastu'[59] etc., 'kśetra-pariśudhi',[60] 'mahābhoga', 'bahu-parivāra-samp-āta',[61] 'sattva-paripāka nirmāṇa'[62] — etc. the collection of all these is called 'kuśala upāyaya' of meritorious effort. By thus differentiating through discrimination proper 'upāyaya' and by properly fulfilling one's own and others' objectives, one does not contract 'samkleśas'[63] just as when mantra-sanctified poison is taken (and no harm comes). And, thus has it been expostulated in the sūtra: "Upāyaya is the knowledge of 'samgrah',[64] 'prajñā' the knowledge of differentiation or discrimination.[65]" It is said in Ārya-śradhā-balādhāna: "What is the skill in upāyaya? It is the acquisition of all dharmas. What is 'prajña'? It is the skill in analysing all dharmas," Both these — 'prajña' and 'upāyaya' and not 'prajña' alone or 'upāyaya' alone have always to be practised even by bodhisattvas who have entered the 'bhūmis',[66] because a bodhisattva's proper conduct in the 'pāramitas' or perfections in all the ten 'bhūmis'[67] has been taught in Daśabhūmika etc.

Of a bodhisattva who roams calmly in the eighth[68] 'bhūmi', 'vyuthāna'[69] (from it) is opposed by the Buddhas. This is understandable when the following (injunction) is studied: "therefore, O jina-putra! of a bodhisattva who is established in this 'achalā'[70] stage and in the collected force of his earlier fixation or 'praṇi-dhāna' and in the fundamental source of dharma,[71] Lord Buddha calls a 'finis' (upasamhāra)[72] to his previously acquired knowledge and He thus addresses him, "well done, well done, O Kulputra! This 'paramārtha kśānti'[73] is for pursuing all Buddha-dharmas. However, O Kulaputra! even so, that intellect which comprises ten 'balas'[74] and four qualifications[75] and is regarded as Buddha dharma's wealth is still not yours. So, yoke yourself into a search for the glory of that Buddha dharma; start effort; do never leave this doorway of 'kśānti', Even then, O Kulaputra! now that you have attained this 'śānti-vimokśa-vihāra'[76] you must think of and own up those ignorance-common folks who, in their restless, disturbed state indulge in varying 'kleśas' and whose minds are clogged with many arguments and counter-arguments. And again, O Kulputra! remember your earlier vows to make available to 'sattvas' a state of no worry through (the cultivation of) true 'jñāna'.[77] This, O Kulaputra! is the dharmatā[78] of all dharmas. Whether or not Tathāgatas[79] are born, this state of 'dharmatā' and 'dharma-dhātu'[80] stays just as 'sarva-dharma śunyatā'[81] and 'sarva-dharmānu-plabdhi',[82] i.e. the emptiness of all phenomena and the non-true existence of all phenomena. Not only are Tathagatas affected by it but even 'śrāvakas' and 'pratyeka-buddhas' attain to this 'avikalpa-dharmatā'[83] or the true nature of 'dharmatā' understanding."

"Again, O kulaputra! observe the inmitable[84] quality of our body, of our 'jñāna', of 'buddha-kśetra', of the accumulation[85] of knowledge, of our aura[86] and of the immaculate purity of speech.[87] You too should generate similar accumulation (of kuśala in various 'bhūmis'). This sole effulgence, O Kulaputra! is the transcendental[88] glow in all dharmas. O Kulaputra! such effulgences of Tathāgatas are infinite,[89] eternally[90] born, eternally-linked,[91] countless, numberless, un-provable, inimitable, matchless. Generate accumulation (of 'kuśala') in order to understand them. Also,

O Kulaputra! observe the illimitable expanse,[92] the illimitable beings[93] and the analysis of illimitable dharma varieties[94] in all the ten directions. Count them and generate Tathāgata's 'abhinirhāra' or kuśala-appropriation in the same manner. O jina-putra! to a bodhisattva who has attained this kind of 'bhūmi', Lord Buddha closes the doors of accumulation ('abhinirhāra') which are prominent, numberless and of unlimited 'jñāna', the abhinirhāra' doors[95] of knowledge through which, by means of the divisions of unlimited knowledge, they generate 'abhinirhāra karma'.[96] O jina-putra! you have to achieve 'adhimukti'[97] you have to achieve 'avabodha'[98] — final release and enlightenment. I commend it to you, jinaputra! I say it to you. If the bodhisattva is not made to enter the doors of the accumulation of 'sarvajnatā-jñāna'[99] he will there (i.e. at that stage) enter 'parinirvāṇa'[100] and the work of all sattvas disintegrate.[101]" Thus has it been propounded in detail. Whatever has been propounded in Ārya Vimala-kirti-nirdeśa and Gayāśirṣa is in contradiction of this, that is, the aforesaid postulate, because it has been dealt with these in a general sense only.

Whatever has been said in Ārya-sarva-dharma-samgrah-vaipulya is also opposite to the above. It is said therein: "O Manjuśri! the 'āvaraṇa'[102] or cover of 'pratikśepa[103] karma' or negating actions of true dharma is very subtle. He who generates 'śobhana[104] sanjñā' or fair cognition and he who generates 'aśobhana[105] sanjñā' or unbecoming cognition in the Tathāgata-propounded dharma, — both retard[106] the true dharma. Such 'dharma-pratikśepa' is tantamount to a rebuttal of Tathāgata." So saying at length, he again said: "O Maitreya! to a person who properly[107] cultivates the Six Perfections for 'a bodhisattva's sambodhi or enlightenment, the ignorant ones will say, 'a bodhisattva should learn only 'prajñā-pāramitā,' what with other perfections?' They regard the other 'upāyaya-pāramitā'[108] as taboo. How do you regard this, O Ajita?[109] Was that Kaśirāja[110] a fool to have given away his flesh in lieu of that of the pigeon to the preying falcon? 'No, my Lord,' said: Maitreya.[111] The Lord said, 'O Maitreya! did those kuśal-mūlas or root-merits (meritorious practices) pertaining to the Six Perfections, which I garnered while practising the conduct of a bodhisattva do me harm?' Maitreya replied, 'not at all, my Lord!' The Lord continued, 'O Ajita! you have practised the proper vows of 'dāna-paramitā' for sixty 'kalpas'.[112] If even you practise 'prajña-pāramitā' for sixty 'kalpas,' those ignorant ones will again say, 'a single 'naya'[113] or path can lead to bodhi; for example, 'śunyatā naya' or the path of emptiness', this has been said in detail. It is also mentioned in Vairochanabhi-sambodhi: 'This 'jñāna' f 'sarvajñatā' has 'karuṇa' or compassion as its root, it is the 'hetu' or cause of 'bodhichitta' and is the end[114] of 'upāyaya'. Therefore, bodhisattvas should always practise both of them."

This also proves that the Tathāgatas are never installed[115] in 'nirvāṇa'. So also the Lord will not stay put in 'nirvāṇa' by accepting the wealth of the fruit of such grand enjoyments: 'rupa-kāyā',[116] 'kśetra'[117] and 'parivāra'[118] attained through the efforts of 'dana' etc.; nor will these be their station in 'samsāra' owing to the total removal of all their delusion,[119] for 'viparyāsa' or delusion alone is the root of cyclic existence. This 'pratipatti' or realisation born of 'prajñā' and 'upāyaya' will aid the stoppage of the consequences[120] of superimposition[121] and contradiction[122] and, give birth to the 'madhyama mārga' or the Middle Way, because 'prajñā' prevents the consequences of superimposition and 'upāyaya' prevents the consequences of contradiction. Hence it is said in Ārya-dharma-samgeeti: 'Lord Buddha's attributes[123] and their expression[124] are conducive to the creation of 'rupa' - kāyā or physical form and not unto the 'abhisamaya'[125] of 'dharma' - kāyā'[126] or subtle form. Again the generation[127] or creation affected by the Tathāgatas through 'prajñā' and 'upāyaya' should be followed or pursued in preference to other factors."

Again, it has been said: "Those who regard dharma as a mere boat should give up dharma too; of course, before that adharma must also be forsaken." This has been said in order that belief in opposing or contrary dharmas is abolished and not that no support be taken for the realisation of the objective. Hence, it has been said: "dharma should be accepted but not stuck[128] to." It means that it should not be accepted from the wrong[129] end or contrary approach. Whatever has been said about the material fruits of 'dāna' etc. has been said only about the 'dāna' practised as aforesaid by people without 'prajñā' and for those who are satisfied with it as such, in order to encourage them to practise further root merit, otherwise, it would go contrary to all that has been earlier said in Ārya-vimala-kirti-nirdeśa etc. Thus it is established that 'prajñā' and 'upāyaya' should both be cultivated. So 'dāna-pāramitā' etc. accompanied by 'prajñā' (wisdom), alone and in no other manner attain an identity, a designation.[130] Therefore, one must strive for the generation of 'prajñā' for sanctifying 'dāna' etc. through absorption in 'samādhi'.[131]

Now, 'śrutamayi[132] prajñā' should be generated first. Through it one grasps the meaning of 'āgama'.[133] Then, through 'chintāmayi[134] prajñā' one pierces or analyses the intelligible[135] and the dubious[136] meanings. Deciding in this manner one should contemplate on real[137] and not unreal[138] connotation, otherwise true cognition or ultimate knowledge will not dawn owing to contemplation on the contrary aspect and non-refutation of doubt.[139] In that case, 'bhāvanā' will become meaningless as in the case of 'tirthikas'.[140] As the Lord has said in Samādhiraja also: "If one perceives 'nairātmya'[141] in all dharmas and, so perceiving, one practises 'bhāvanā' or meditation, it will become the 'hetu' or cause of nirvāṇa-fruit; other causes are no-wise for 'śānti' or peace."

Hence, by means of contemplative wisdom and analysis through logic and scriptures, one must meditate on the true nature of 'bhūtas'. That all things, in the ultimate sense, are non-existent[142] has been concluded on the basis of logic and scriptures. As has been stated in the scripture called, Ārya-dharma-samgīti: "non-generation alone is true; other dharmas like generation[143] are not true." It is stated as being in accordance with 'paramārtha' or the ultimate meaning. Non-generation (i.e. non-true existence) is true. However, in the ultimate analysis, there is neither 'utpāda' (generation or being) nor 'anutpāda' (non-generation or non-being), because that or 'paramārtha' is beyond all classification or label. Again, it is said in the same scripture: "O kulputra! the attitude or position of the world is dependent on relying[144] on 'utpāda' (generation or being) and 'nirodha' or cessation' (non-being). Therefore, the supremely compassionate Tathāgata, in order to abolish the world's areas of fear had said for practical reasons, that 'there is birth, there is cessation', and certainly not (for the reason) that, in the ultimate sense, any dharma is born." It is stated in Ārya-Buddha-samgīti also: "What is the query about 'yoniśa',[145] what 'yoni?'[146] It has been said that non-generation is 'yoni' and the query about it is 'yoniśa prichhā."[147] And, again: all dharmas are 'chakāra[148] mukha' because they are without beginning without cessation; also, all dharmas are 'abhāva-mukha'[149] because they are void or empty by nature."

Ārya-satya-dvya-vibhāga also states: "the commonality of 'anutpāda' or non-generation is the commonality of all dharmas or phenomena." Prajñā-pāramita says: "O Subhuti, form is devoid of the 'svabhāva' (self-existence) of form just as the bounds of 'vijñāna' (discriminatory cognition) are devoid of the (true) self-existence or svabhāva of 'vijñāna' owing to the emptiness of all self-nature." Hastika-kśya also states: "nothing exists whose generation or birth is possible. Ignorant people look for the possible from the impossible dharmas." It has been said in Pitā-putra-samāgama: "all dharmas during the three times (past, present and future) have been identical. All dharmas were 'svabhāva-rahita' or without true self-existence in the past and are so in the present also." Thus should it be examined through 'āgama' (scriptures). It is not possible for others to refute such conclusions from the scriptures through logic established. So, examining through logic must be done.

Now about logic, briefly. Is the generation of 'bhāvas' (things, phenomena, etc.) without cause or with cause? It cannot be without cause because it is occasionally noticeable. In the absence of any reliance on 'kāraṇa' or cause and because of the (intervening) interval, why should not things generate (themselves) always and everywhere as if in 'utpāda-kāla' or an era of creation? If there is no interval from the time of non-generation, there will be no generation (of things) even at the time of generation. Thus there is no generation without cause. There is no generation with cause either. There can be no creation or bẹing from an imaginary, permanent 'hetu' like an 'īśwara'[150] as believed by tirthikas' (heretics) because creation is noticeable (as occurring) at intervals ('kramaśa'). Of 'avikala'[151] or constant causes the result cannot be occasional owing to its nirapeksattvatā[152] or (independent) constancy. 'Iśwara', etc. being self-competent need not depend on any other (cause) for assistance as he is permanent. There need be no dependence for the independent. These 'īśwara' etc. being devoid of omnipotence are non-existent in essence like the son of a barren woman. A thing having capacity for 'artha-kriyā'[153] is incapable of generating any act in an occasional sequence as has been already discussed. There is no simultaneous creation either, because, by creating everything at the same time, if it can repeat such creation later on also then, owing to a repetition of its omnipotent nature, there will arise the possibility of the creation of things as before. If there is no repetition and the previous nature is abandoned, the possibility of 'anityatā' or impermanence would arise.

Hence, nothing by the designation of 'nitya' or permanent exists. The Lord has said, "There is a superimposition[154] of 'asata'[155] (the non-existent). Belief in such artificial or non-existent things as 'ākāśa',[156] 'nirodh'[157] and nirvāṇa (space, cessation and release), etc. is superimposition." Therefore, there is none of the creation or 'utpāda' from 'nitya' or permanence; neither is there any from 'anitya' or impermanence, because owing to the nothingness of these during the past and the future no creation is possible from them; otherwise too, it would be a creation without cause or 'hetu'? As there is no creation in similar or dissimilar times, there can be no creation from the present time also. Thus there is no simultaneity of generating time; otherwise, for causal reasons, it will give rise to simultaneity of generation or creation also. There is no generation from variation in time either, because if it takes place — after a difference in time, there could be generation in the past also. If, in regarding creation as from 'avyavadhāna'[158] or non-interval, interval occurs, all 'kśaṇas' or moments will merge into one 'kśaṇa'[159] and, in consequence, a 'kalpa' will (also) squeeze into 'kśaṇa' just as the linking of atoms in all directions will reduce the 'pinda'[160] or mass also to a mere atom. Linkage with a single part makes a moment alive (sāvayava).[161] Things are not self-created either owing to this premise being at par with the non-cause postulate and the concept of the creator being self-contradictory. There is no possibility of generating from both because of the conjunction of the drawbacks of both postulates.

Hence things are without any substantial existence, i.e. unrelated in the ultimate sense. This is not contrary to the (teachings of) scriptures even though in an apparent or illusory sense, creation does appear to exist. So the Lord has said: 'Things exist only in 'samvrita' and not 'paramārtha'; The delusion about the 'nissvabhāva' of things is called the 'samvriti satya'.[162]

Such-like logic has also been endorsed by the Lord in sūtras like Śālistamba? By itself, from another or from both and without cause, there can be no creation.

Now, let us examine by another argument. 'Bhāvas' are of two kinds; with form and without form. Of these, pitcher, etc. which have form are not of one 'svabhāva' (entity, nature) being composed of different atoms. Being situated fore and aft and when divided into directions like east, etc. the atom's existence is not established. And, being in (a state of) conglomeration, they cannot be said to possess different self-existence or 'svabhāva'. There is no other existence of a thing barring single (existence) and multiple (existence). Therefore, things with form are 'nissabhāva' or non-existent in the ultimate sense like a form seen in a dream. This has been stated by the Lord in Ārya Lankāvatāra: "O mahāmati (the greatly wise); even the horns of a cow, when divided into atoms, do not exist. Even atoms cannot retain atomic qualities or characteristics when divided."

Things which are without form are equally non-existent (in essence), when similarly examined. So also things outwardly appearing as blue etc. though not truly existent are only 'vijñāna skandha'[163] or an aggregate of cognition, though without form but appearing as blue. The Lord has said, "there are no apparent forms; only the mind sees itself (i.e. its own superimposed reflection)." Therefore, the blue etc. being seen in different shapes and because of the received and the recepient being incapable of the same existing nature as a consequence of the contradiction between the one and the many, the 'one' cannot be of the nature of 'many'. When the non-existence of the one is proved, the existence of the many is also impossible, because the 'many' is only a conglomeration of the 'one's'.

If these manifestations of form etc. are false[164] or insubstantial and are accepted as such, 'vijñāna' itself will become false because the cognition of the form will be no different from form itself. 'Vijñāna' or cognition has no other form apart from its own manifest form. Forms etc. do not shine by themselves but when they are cognised as false, cognition itself becomes false. That is why the Lord has said: "all cognition is māyā or illusory".[165] So the one and the many being non-existent are not true in the ultimate sense. The Lord has said this very thing in Lankāvatāra: "The nature of things is like the reflection in a mirror which is devoid of both singularity and plurality; although it (i.e. the reflection) appears to be there but, in fact, it is not there." Devoid of 'ekattva' or singularity and 'anyattva' or multiplicity, it is neither one nor many. 'Buddhi' or intellect does not take over the nature of existence of that which it examines. Therefore, these are said to be 'nirabhilāśa'[166] and 'nissvabhāva' i.e. unbiased and without essence."

By determining the (true) meaning of things in this manner through deliberative intellect one must generate meditative wisdom in order to manifest the true meaning of things. It has been said in sūtras like Ārya-ratna-megha: "the true meaning never becomes manifest or clear merely through listening (to a lot of expositions). Experience comes only to such as those who practise 'pratipatti',[167] or through comprehension. The cover of darkness lying over the 'samyaka' or true meaning cannot be removed without the dawn of the clear light of 'jñāna'. If meditation is done profusely the clear knowledge of the hidden meaning is also born. If 'jñāna' comes to those who contemplate on 'aśubha' and 'prithvi-kritsna'[168] only, what then to speak of those who meditate on 'bhūtas'!" The success of meditation as the harbinger of the fruit of true knowledge has been described in Ārya-samādharāja: "I tell you, I put it across to you that as much as a person may analyse or indulge in logic so much will his mind be moulded in accordance with the conclusion he arrives at." This has been said in detail. Hence, he who wants to manifest truth or wishes to grasp the essence of things should practise 'bhāvanā'; — meditation.

Herein, the yogi should first cultivate 'śamatha'[169] or calm in order to stabilise the mind. Being 'chanchala' or flippant like water, the mind cannot become poised without the basis of 'śamatha'. Nor can a person whose mind is not 'samāhita'[170] or tranquil can understand the truth of things ('yathā bhūtama'), the essence. The Lord said, "one with a tranquil mind understands the 'yathā-bhūta'. Tranquillity comes quickly to a person indifferent towards the desire for gain etc. and to one who is of correct disposition, is of the nature of dukha-awareness[171] etc. and is on the path of 'veerya'[172] or effort. Hence 'dāna' etc. have been mentioned repeatedly in Ārya-sandhi-nirmochana etc.

Thus staying in 'śamatha' collections like 'śila'[173] etc., bowing to all Buddhas and bodhisattvas at a spot convenient to the mind after indicating 'pāpa'[174] and commending 'punya',[175] keeping in view 'mahākaruṇa' which aims at the welfare of the entire world, with body erect (but at ease), sitting on a congenial seat (or in the comfortable posture of 'sukhāsana')[176] assuming the lotus pose, one should practise 'samādhi' or meditational repose.

First of all mind should be briefly fixed on all aspects of the object of contemplation so that it becomes a solid or massed object (to reflect on). In brief, an object is of two kinds: with form and without form. In order to ward off the defect of deviation[177] of an ādikarmika' or novice initiate, it is proper to have a small or brief 'ālambana'[178] only. When one has mastered 'manaskāra' or mental actualisation one can take to a larger or detailed 'ālambana' by refining or rectifying the process through the differentiations of 'skandha' and 'dhātu' etc. As has been said in Ārya-samādhi-nirmochana etc.: "the yogis have many kinds of 'ālambanas' like the eighteen types of 'śunyatā'.[179]

Here also, for the good of sentient beings, the Lord has spoken about 'vastubheda'[180] in 'abhidharma'[181] etc. in accordance with the differences between the formless (vastu or thing) and the corporeal (things) in brief, medium and detailed manners. For the removal of superimpositions and falsities, the thing or the object should be regarded as a mere mass or collection of 'skandha' and 'dhatu'. Thus being assured of the collection with respect to all things, the mind should again and again be brought around to concentrate on that (massed aspect of things).

In case the mind, in between, deviates and gets outward-prone due to 'rāga' or attachment, one must silence such aberration by reflecting on the 'aśubha' or unwholesome (responsible for deviation) and stabilise the mind again and again. The sequence of reflection on 'aśubha' has not been mentioned here in detail for fear of dilation. When the mind appears to be disinterested, one should reflect on the advantages of meditation and concentrate on one's interest on it. Whenever faults of deviation or distraction appear, one must quieten down one's disinterestedness. When owing to having been overcome by 'styāna'[182] and 'middha',[183] one's mind does not get clearly absorbed in holding on to the prop or 'ālambana', then either through contemplation ('bhāvanā') on a luminous cognition ('āloks samjñā') or through a mental visualisation of a supremely joyous object like Buddha etc. and by so calming down 'laya' or mental lethargy, one should again firmly hold on to the 'ālambana'.

When the mind looks naughty in between through some remembrance of a previous joy or enjoyment one should reflect on the 'samvega'[184] of 'anityatā' or transitoriness and calm down its naughtiness. Then, one must try to persuade the mind towards that very prop (ālambana) without 'abhisamskāra'[185] or variation.

When the mind, shorn of both lethargy and insolence appears to be properly engaged of its own volition,[186] then, through suspension of 'ābhoga'[187] or effort, detachment should be practised. When 'satyābhoga'[188] or true effort (after pacifying 'laxity etc.) is practised in a state of 'sama-pravritti'[189] or balance, 'vikśepa'[190] or mental confusion (i.e. complicated samadhi-state) occurs, (i.e. the mind is disturbed).

When the mind, without 'abhisamskāra' or variation and of its own volition, becomes engaged in that very 'ālambana' one should consider 'śamatha' or abiding calm as achieved. The nature of 'śamatha' is the one-pointedness of the mind, a characteristic common to all types of tranquillity, its 'ālambana' is not fixed, though. The Lord has spoken of this path in Ārya-prajñāpāramita etc. also. He says, "(the sekeer) fixes ('sthāpita') his mind there, establishes ('samsthāpita') it, pinpoints ('avasthāpita') it, houses ('upasthāpita') it, controls ('damana') it, calms ('śānta') it, stills ('vyupaśānta') it, concentrates ('ekāgra') and rests in meditative equipose ('śamāhita')". Thus described in nine nomenclatures.

Now, here 'sthāpayati' means 'binds the mind to the

'ālambana': 'samsthāpayati' means 'to engage the mind to that prop or 'ālambana' systematically; 'avasthāpayati' means 'on discovering confusion, removes it; 'upa-sthāpayati means 'again fixes the mind to that very 'ālambana' after removing 'vikśepa'; 'damayati' means 'generates 'rati' or desire for the prop; 'śāmayati' means 'subdues 'a-rati' or non-desire (for ālambana) after observing the faults of 'vikśepa' (deviation)'; 'vyupasāmayati' means, 'calms down indolence and do-nothing-ness that have crept in', 'ekoti-karoti' means 'tries to enter the 'ālambana' without 'abhisamskāra'; 'samādadhāti' means 'practises 'upekśā' after attaining tranquillity of mind or 'chitta-samatā', that is, practises withdrawal from the world or 'samanvākaraṇa'.[191] These are the meanings (of the above terms) as given by Ārya Maitreya and by former āchāryas.

Briefly speaking, all samadhis have six faults:[192] sloth,[193] forsaking the 'ālambana'[194] mental lethargy,[195] insolence,[196] non-effort[197] and effort.[198] To overcome or wipe out these 'doṣas' one must meditate on the eight eraser-samskāras,[199] which are faith,[200] desire to act,[201] industriousness,[202] alacrity,[203] non-forgetfulness,[204] alertness,[205] mental refinement[206] and equanimity.[207] Of these, the first four are an antidote to 'kausidya' or sloth. Thus, through 'śraddhā' or faith, accompanied by indications of the generation of correct knowledge[208] of the efficacy of samādhi, the yogi's will to practise it is born; from will or desire ('abhilaṣā) one should commence the cultivation of 'veerya' or effort Through effort one attains bodily and mental activity. Activeness of body and mind removes slothfulness. Therefore, 'śraddhā' etc. should be contemplated upon for the sake of warding off 'kausīdya' or sloth etc. 'Smriti' or non-forgetfulness is the opposite of the giving up of 'ālambana'. 'Samprajñaya' or awareness is the opposite of mental lethargy and insolence, because it clearly exposes the reality of both. If mental lethargy and insolence are not subdued, the fault of 'anābhoga'[209] accurs. As opposite to it, 'chetanā' or mental alertness should be contemplated upon. When mental sloth and insolence are romoved and the mind becomes calm, the fault of 'ābhoga'[210] accurs. To oppose it, one must contemplate on 'upekśa' or detachment.

Samādhi, comprising these eight eraser samskāras, is most efficacious. It generates qualities like 'riddhi'[211] etc. Hence it is said in sūtra: "a person equipped with the eight eraser samskāras contemplates on the state of 'riddhi'. Such concentration of the mind accompanied by more and more of activity[212] with the association of such qualities or 'guṇas' as 'ālambana' attains the designation of 'dhyāna', 'arupi-samāpatti'[213] and 'vimokśa'.[214]

In this manner when 'upeksa' or detachment is accompanied by 'vedanā'[215] or awareness and becomes rational and meaningful it is called 'anāgamya',[216] inaccessible or un-definable, because 'chitta' or mind is the 'prayoga' or subject of the First Dhyāna.[217] To be free from 'kāma trişnā' (hankering after desires) and 'pāpa-dharma' (evil proclivities of the mind), to keep linked with logic, reflectiveness, joy, happiness and inner bliss is designated as First Dhyāna. Also, the first dhyāna being devoid of 'vitarka' is called 'dhyānantara' or mid-dhyāna. When it is without 'vichāra' or reflection and 'vitarka' or reason and becomes free from the desire of staying in the First Dhyāna stage, is accompanied by the bliss of the joy of devotion and of spirituality, it is called Second Dhyāna. When it becomes free from the desire of staying in the Second Dhyāna stage and accompanied by joy, detachment, recollectedness and awareness — 'sukha' 'upekśa', 'smriti' and 'samprajanyā' — it is called Third Dhyāna. When it is free from the desire of staying in the Third Dhyāna stage and is accompanied by non-dukha, non-sukha feelings, 'upekśa and 'smriti', it is called Fourth Dhyāna. Thus, the mind should be linked with 'arupya smāpatti' or formless meditation and dominant[218] 'āyatanas'[219] or entrances of release etc. in accordance with the distinctions of 'ālambana' and 'ākāra'[220] or form.

So, after stabilizing the mind in the 'ālambana', one should analyse with (discriminating) wisdom so that, through the bliss of the dawn of the light of 'jñāna', the seed of the delusion is totally eradicated; otherwise, as in the case if 'tirthikas', there can be no removal of kleśas merely through 'samādhi'. As has been said in Samādhirāja-sūtra: "bhāvanā' may be practised in such samādhi but it will not spell the loss of 'ātma-samjñā'[221] or body-consciousness. It will again agitate the 'kleśas' as during 'undreka[222] samādhi' bhāvanā or over-mentalisation in meditational process."

'Prajñā-bhāvanā-krama' or the sequence of meditation on 'prajñā has been briefly indicated in Ārya Lankāvatāra: "on taking to the 'chitta-mātra'[223] (path), one should not dwell in 'bāhyārtha' or only apparent meaning (of phenomenon); by stabilizing oneself on the 'ālambana' of 'tathatā'[224] one should go beyond the bounds of 'mind only'. After crossing over the mind only path one should go beyond the 'nirābhāsa'.[225]" The yogi who stays in the 'nirābhāsa' or a state 'of non-fallacious appearances' will see 'mahayāna'. Purified by 'praṇidhāna' or vows, the state of satiety is stilled. One cannot experience the noble non-soul[226] soul 'jñāna' in a state of 'nirābhāsa'.

This is what the aforesaid means: at first the yogi should reflect over those external meanings which have been superimposed by others over dharmas with form, that is, whether they are different from cognition ('vijñāna') or that they are vijñāna itself appearing as such as if in the dream state. Then, he should consider them with respect to their atoms in accordance with 'vijñāna; observing the atoms in their parts, the yogi will not find those superimposed meanings. Not finding them there, he will so conclude that all this is mind only and that there is no external meaning or substance at all. Therefore, it has been said: "one should not imagine external meanings on ascending the mind-only path". That is, one must give up 'vikalpas' or superimposed nomenclatures of dharmas with form. To reflect on those 'bhāvas' or phenomena with apparent or super-imposed meanings leads to the disappearance of those meanings.

Having thus reflected over dharmas with form, one should analyse dharmas without form. One who remains only a 'chitta-mātrin' cannot become a 'grāhaka' or receiver in the absence of that which could be the 'grāhya' or the receivable as the recepient has always to depend on an object which is to be received. Therefore, it must be concluded that the mind is devoid of the functions of the both the 'grāhya' and the 'grāhaka'; it is 'advya' or non-dual. 'Advya' is defined as "sticking on to the prop of 'tathatā', one must go beyond the 'chittmātra' stage too". The attitude of the 'receiver' should be over-stepped. It means that the non-cognisance of duality should be based on the knowledge of duality.

In this manner, after crossing over the 'chitta-mātra' stage, one should also go beyond the non-dual cognition stage, because there is no generation of 'bhāvas' either by themselves or through another agent and the 'grāhya' and the grāhaka' are illusionary, non-existent. Because they are dissimilar[227] from what they appear, their truth or reality is also not opposite. In 'advya jñāna'[228] or non-dual comprehension also, the feeling of existence in substance should be abandoned which means that one should stay in the 'nirābhāsa jñāna' or non-apparent knowledge of 'advya' or non-duality. By so doing, the mind gets stabilized in the realisation of the 'nissvabhāvatā' of all dharmas. Such a person, owing to his access to the 'paramatattva' or the ultimate essence (of things), enters 'nirvikalpa samādhi' or immaculate absorption.

When the yogi is established in the 'nirābhāsa jñāna of the non-dual cognition he also gets established in the 'paramtattva'[229] — the ultimate or supreme essence (reality); he sees 'mahāyāna'. Realising the 'paramatattva' is called Mahāyāna. His 'paramtattva darśana' or experiencing the ultimate reality is this that, analysing all dharmas or phenomena with the eye of 'prajñā', he sees the truth in the light of 'samyaka jñāna'[230] or ultimate knowledge. So it is said in the sūtra: "what is 'parmārtha darśanama' or seeing the supreme or ultimate truth of things? (it is) the non-seeing of all dharmas." Herein is indicated such type of 'non-seeing' (as described above) and not the non-seeing (blindness) or ignorance of those who, with eyes shut like the born blind, see nothing owing to the bafflement[231] of 'pratyayas' and non-mentalisation of phenomena.

The yogi will remain in bondage, like a person who has arisen from 'asañjyi' samāpatti',[232] owing to the non-removal of 'vāsanā' or desire for fixation in things born of contrariety ('viparyāsa'), because in 'bhāvas' themselves are created the basic fixations of the 'kleśa' mass or mental defilements of 'rāga'[233] (attachment, addiction) etc.: It has been said in Ārya-satya-dvaya-nirdeśa etc.: "the root of 'rāga' etc. is fixation in 'bhāvas'," What has been said in Avikalpa-praveśa-dhārani etc. (about the yogi 'stopping through non-mentalisation such things as the objects of form etc. refers to that 'anupalabdhi' (absence of substantial existence) which comes only through an examination with 'prajñā' and the non-mentalisation of that alone; it does not merely refer to the absence of mentalisation. Fixation in 'rūpa' or form etc., which has been there from time immemorial, cannot be eradicated, like 'asanjñi samapātti' etc. merely by abandoning mentalisation."

It is not possible to remove the 'manasikāra' or mentalisation generated by previous 'abhiniveśa' or fixations in 'rūpa' (form) etc. without the removal of doubts just as there can be no extinction of the fact of burning unless fire is removed. It is not possible to take out these false 'vikalpas' or contrary alternatives of form etc. from the mind as though plucking out a thorn with our own hands. How, then (to do it)? (It is done) by removing the seeds of doubt. The yogi, after examining through the eyes of 'prajñā' these seeds of doubt and their formerly acquired form etc. and such as those whose non-acquiredness is experienced in the moment of acquirement, can of course remove them like the cognition of the serpent in the rope and in no other manner. Similarly, when the seed of doubt is removed, one can abandon the mentalisation of the objects of form etc. also and in no other manner. Were it not so then, in the absence of the glow of samādhi and not seen even by the eye of wisdom, the yogi's doubt about the existence of form etc. is not removed like that of a person in a blind well (of ignorance) feeling doubts about the pots etc. lying in the house. When such doubt is not removed, he will become a person whose 'timir-doṣa'[234] or clouded eyesight is not removed and who remains susceptible to fixation in false insubstantial forms, which cannot be castigated by anyone. Therefore, by clasping the mind with the hand of 'samādhi' and with the help of the very subtle weapon of 'prajñā' one should eradicate the seeds of the disease of false 'vikalpas' or alternatives present in the mind; just as uprooted trees do not again take root in the earth so also will false 'vikalpas' be not born in the mind. Hence, in order to remove the 'āvaraṇa' or the overlying crust of false appearances the Lord has pointed out the 'yuganadha[235]-vāhi-mārga (two-fold single path) of 'śamatha' (equipoise) and 'vipaśyanā' (insight), because "these two are the cause of absolute knowledge ('avikalpa-jñāna')." As is said in the sūtra: "Samādhi is attained through staying in 'Śila'; through samādhi comes 'prajñā bhāvanā or contemplation on wisdom; through 'prajñā' comes absolute knowledge; a person with absolute knowledge attains the wealth of 'Śila'."

In this manner, when the mind has been stabilized in the 'ālambana' through equipoise ('śamatha'), the glow of ultimate 'jñāna' is born after deliberation through 'prajñā'. When this glow shines, the cover (āvaraṇa) is lifted like the disappearance of darkness. Therefore, both these 'śamatha' and prajñā', like the eye and the light, are mutually beneficial in the generation of right knowledge. There is no contradiction between the two as between light and darkness inspite of the difference in their 'guṇas' or characteristics. 'Samādhi' is not of the nature of darkness. What is it, then? It is of the nature of the concentration of mind. "Being in equipoise, it knows the reality (of things)." In accordance with this assertion, it i.e. 'samādhi' gets totally identified with 'prajñā'; it is not contradictory to it. When a 'samāhita' or a person of staid mind examines with his 'prajñā' there will be no acquirement[236] of all dharmas. That, in itself, is the supreme non-acquirement[237] or perception. Such a staidness[238] indicating stage of the yogi is (a state of) 'anābhoga'[239] or total-satiety, because nothing beyond it remains to be experienced. 'Śānta' or tranquil (state) is the cessation of all such contrary frauds[240] as those of 'bhāva'[241] or is-ness and 'abhāva'[242] or is-not-ness.

Thus, when the yogi does not find any inherent existence of things after examining through 'prajñā' (wisdom), he experiences no contrariety of 'bhāvas' nor does he experience the 'vikalpa' of 'abhāva'. If is-ness or 'bhāva' is noticed anywhere, its stoppage or cessation will produce an alternative (vikalpa'). However, if by examining through 'prajñā' the yogi discovers no is-ness of things in the three[243] times, how can there be any opposing alternative of the same as is-not-ness or 'abhāva'? So, other 'vikalpas' also will not touch him owing to the permeableness[244] of 'vikalpas' of 'bhāva' and 'abhāva'. There can be no 'vyāpaka'[245] or a permeable[246] entity. So, this is the supreme immaculate yoga. For a yogi stabilized in that (i.e. immaculate yoga) all contradictions or alternatives having been eradicated, his 'jñeyāvaraṇa'[247] or cover of cognition and 'klesāvaraṇa'[248] or cover of mental defilement are totally destroyed. It has been said in Ārya satya-dvya nirdeśa etc. also that the root of 'kleśāvaraṇa' is the superimposition of 'bhāva' etc. on uncreated, non-existent things or phenomena.

Through this yoga practice by removing all contrarities of 'is-ness', all contradictions of 'is-ness' etc., the ignorance-natured roots of 'kleśāvaraṇas' are totally destroyed. As has been stated in Arya satya-dvaya nirdeśa: "O Manjuśri! how can 'kleśa' or mental defilement be suppressed?" How are 'kleśas' discovered?' Manjuśri replied, 'in the ultimate sense, there is a false superimposition (on things) through 'samvrita'[249] or the apparent over totally unborn, uncreated and non-existent dharmas. This false superimposition gives rise to 'samkalpa' and 'vikalpa'[250] premise and counter-premise; 'sankalpa' and 'vikalpa' give rise to 'ayoniśa mansikāra'[251] or un-meditational mentalisation, which gives rise to 'ātma-samāropa' or the superimposition of a self (or entity on phenomena); 'ātma-samāropa' gives rise to 'driṣṭi-paryuthhāna'[252] or sight distraction; this sight-distraction generates 'kleśaś. O devaputra! in the ultimate sense, he alone is un-superimposed who realises all dharmas to be totally unborn, uncreated. He who, in the ultimate sense, is un-superimposed is without 'vikalpa'. He who is free from 'vikalpa' is meditationally balanced. He who is meditationally balanced can never have self-superimposition. He who is free from the superimposition of a self does not suffer from 'dhyāna pariyuthhāna'. In the ultimate sense, 'dristi-paryuthhāna' or sight-distraction does not take place till one sees 'nirvāṇa'. So his 'kleśa' must be seen as 'vineeta' or highly subdued, staid as he is in the 'anutpāda' or uncreated realm. Such a one is called 'kleśa-vinaya' or one with subdued defilements. O devaputra! when he, through his 'nirābhāsa jnāña' or knowledge bereft of (fallacious) appearances (knowledge of emptiness), realises to be totally void, non-existent and uncreated in the ultimate sense, he, O devaputra! understands the 'kleśas'. The rogue who knows the class of the serpent will also cure the venom of the serpent. Similarly, O devaputra! he who thoroughly understands the 'gotra' or class of 'kleśas', his kleśas are removed, become 'śānta' (quiet)." Devaputra said, "O Manjuśri! What is the 'gotra' of 'klesas'?" Manjuśri replied, "O devaputra! all superimpositions on dharmas, which are totally unborn, uncreated and non-existent in the ultimate sense are the 'gotras' (classes, castes) of 'kleśas'." Thus stated at length.

When 'bhāvas' etc. are overthrown, and because 'viparyāsa'[253] or contrariety is all-pervasive, with this overthrow all contrary 'āvarṇas' are also overthrown and the cognitive cover will also be adequately removed because 'āvarṇas' are of the quality of contrariety. With removal of the cognitive cover and impediment removed the glow of 'jñāna' spreads in front of the yogi like a ray of the sun spreading speedily all over a cloudless sky. Thus, 'vijñāna'[254] (consciousness, cognitive knowledge) is, by nature, effulgent but that effulgence does not shine forth owing to impediments. Un-hindered, why will not that 'subtle (achintya)',[255] with its especial capacity regained, not illumine everything as such? Therefore, 'sarvajñatā' is attained by obtaining the true knowledge of things in both the apparent ('samvrita') and the ultimate ('paramārtha') sense. So, this is the supreme path for the removal of 'āvarṇas' and the attainment of 'sarvajñatā'.

In the 'śrāvaka' path etc., owing to the non-eradication of all the contrarities ('viparyāsa'), the two 'āvaraṇas' are not properly removed. As has been said in Ārya-Lankā-vatāra etc.: "other people get to know 'nirvāṇa' by observing all dharmas as subject to 'hetu' or cause; however, O mahāmati! they cannot attain emancipation ('mokśa'), because they do not realise the non-self nature of dharmas. O mahāmati (greatly wise)! a person in śrāvaka-yāna possessing an intellect which stays in the experience of correct[256] 'satyas' attains release[257] even in non-release.[258] O mahāmati! here one must try to avert[259] faulty vision[260] or outlook (i.e. adherence to wrong doctrine)." As there is no 'mokśa' through other vehicles, the Lord has here said, "there is only one vehicle."

Paths like 'śrāvaka-yāna' etc. have been propounded only by the ignorant for the instruction of the ignorant, such (things) as that 'skandhas'[261] etc. are only dharmas and there is no 'self' (ātmā). So thinking, a 'śrāvaka' enters 'pudgala nairātmya',[262] the non-self concept of a thing; that the threefold[263] 'dhātu'-division of the world is only 'vijñapti'[264] (mental phenomena); so thinking, he enters the 'nairātmya' of a vijñānavādin,[265] which deals only with 'bāhyārtha' or apparent phenomena. Now, by his entering the 'nairātmya' or non-self aspect of non-dual (advya) knowledge in the aforesaid manner, he enters the 'paramatattva' or the supreme truth of things. Entering the supreme truth is not merely entering mental cognition ('vijñapti'). It has been said in Ārya-lokottara-parva. "Moreover, O Jinaputra! 'traidhātuka' manifests in the 'chitta-mātra' and that mind also appears in the shape of 'ananta-madhyataya' (without an end, without a middle). The (two) 'antas'[266] (ends) being of the quality of generation[267] and dissolution and the 'madhya'(middle) being devoid of the quality of staying, the mind is 'ananta-madhya', i.e. without ends, without middle". Therefore, to enter the non-dual 'jñāna' is to enter the 'tattva,' the reality of things."

If it is asked: "how does a yogi's state get so refined?", the answer is: 'it is refined by 'praṇidhāna' or the vow to tread the road to the goal'. The vow that the bodhisattvas have taken to serve all sentient beings through 'mahākaruṇā', by practising more and more of such 'kuśalas' as 'dāna' etc., on the strength of that vow, the yogi's state will become refined. So long as the dependence on all beings is not eradicated even after the realisation of the 'nissvabhāvatā' of all dharmas, he continues to be in 'samsāra' till the end, being engrossed with the faults of the cyclic round ('samsāra').

How is this supreme knowledge full of total satiety and tranquillity? The reason for its being so is stated below: (the yogi) sees the noble 'nirātma jñāna' through, 'nirābhasa' or a non-fallacious view of things.' Therefore, the noble non-dual 'jñāna', which is acceptable to the non-dualists in the ultimate sense, is also non-self (nairātmya'). The yogi sees the 'nissvabhāva' through his knowledge of the 'advya nirābhasa' or non-dual, non-fallacious meditation experience. Afterwards, it becomes total satiety ('anābhoga') because nothing else remains to be seen and it is called 'śānta' (still, calm) because of the absence of any 'vikalpa' or contradiction.

Now, here it may be asked: "What yogi is such as 'sees'?" (The answer is): in the 'paramārtha' or ultimate sense no self ('ātmā') etc. has an independent entity nor does the yogi 'see' anything. However, in the 'samvrita' or apparent sense, just as, with the mere generation of the knowledge of the form of things with form, it is only cognition (vijñāna) which appears in these different forms like one seeing a Deva-datta or a Yajña-datta through cognition (of their forms); there is no such thing as a self. So also here the yogi sees the generation of 'advya nirābhāsa jñāna' or the non-dual non-fallacious knowledge. Thus said: "In spite of all dharmas being non-existent in the ultimate sense, awareness of 'samvriti' is not undesirable whether it is a common person or a yogi". As has been stated at length in 'Āryasatya-dvaya nirdeśa': it is, in the ultimate sense, totally non-existent but even so it seeks the way through 'samvriti', apparent truth.

What about the order of 'śrāvakas', 'pratyeka-buddhas', 'bodhisattvas', Buddhas and the common people, then? That which has no 'kāraṇa' (cause) in 'samvriti' (the apparent) is unborn even in 'samvriti' as in the case of the horns of a hare etc. That which has a cause must be born even though it may not be true in the ultimate sense just as an illusion, a reflection, an echo. Owing to their being un-analysable, illusion etc. inspite of their dependent origination[268] in the 'samvriti', are not truly existent in the ultimate sense. Therefore, the entire 'jagata'[269] has been designated as 'māyā' or illusion. Just as the illusion of birth takes place in the case of sentient beings because of the illusion of 'kleśas' and 'karma', so also 'jñāna māyā'[270] or the illusion of knowledge envelops the yogis because of the illusion of the accumulation of 'punya' (virtue) and 'jñāna' (knowledge). As has been said in Ārya-prajña-pāramitā "O Subhuti! thus all dharmas are 'nirmāṇa'(conjectured creation). Some are created by 'srāvakas', some by 'pratyeka-buddhas', some by 'kleśas' and some by 'karmas'. In this manner, O Subhuti! all dharmas are 'nirmita',[271] of conjectured existence." The difference between the yogis and the common people is that the former do not regard that illusion to be true, because like the illusion-maker magician they know all illusions as such; that's why they are called yogis. Those who are foolish like the common people take that frivolous[272] play to be the truth and, because of their belief in the contrary, are called ignorant. It has been said in Ārya-dharma-sangiti: "Just as a magician tries to seek release from (the idea of) creation (of his illusion), he does not feel any attachment (for his māyā-creation), because he knows it (to be illusory) from the very beginning. The person who has attained true enlightenment,[273] knowing 'tri-bhāva'[274] to be only illusory, puts on a guise for the world while already aware of the reality of the world ('jagata')."

The 'tattva' (of all dharmas) should be meditated upon in this sequence.

When mental lethargy ('laya') and excitement ('audhatya') arise during meditation, they should be quietened down as before. The two-fold single path of 'śamatha' and 'vipaśyanā' tranquillity and perceptive insight — is completed when 'jñāna', shorn of 'laya' and 'audhatya', enters 'anabhisamskāra'[275] (immaculate) state with the 'ālambana' of the 'nissvābhavatā of all dharmas. And, as long as possible, the practitioner should stay in the 'adhimukti bhūmi'[276] through the force of 'adhimukti'[277] and 'śaraṇā-gama', — faith and devotion. After this, without giving up the lotus posture, the practitioner may, if desired, contemplate as under in the 'vyuthhāna' or rising-up state: 'If all these dharmas are 'nissvābhava' or insubstantial in the ultimate sense, do they still exist in the 'samvriti' (apparent) aspect?' It has been said in Arya-ratna-megha: how does a bodhisattva become proficient in 'nairātmya' (non-self doctrine)? O Kulaputra! the bodhisattva examines 'rūpa' (form) with right wisdom, examines 'vedanā'[278] (feeling), 'sanjñā'[279] (cognition) and 'samskāra'[280] and observing these forms, he does not notice any generation of form, does not find cessation ('nirodha'),[281] does not find 'samudāya'[282] (aggregation). This is due to the establish-ment of his 'prajñā' or wisdom in 'paramārtha' and not because of his natural wont." This has been stated in detail. However, the ignorant persons, by attributing a false substantiality to non-existent things, continue to wander in cyclic rounds, experiencing countless dukhas. Keeping this in mind and addressing 'mahākaruṇā' one must reflect: 'I shall do that by which I may attain the true knowledge of all dharmas so that I could instruct these (ignorant) persons in 'dharmatā' (the true nature of dharmas, which is emptiness)'.

After offering worship and prayers to all the Buddhas and bodhisattvas, one should undertake the great vow ('mahā-praṇidhāna') of noble, virtuous conduct ('bhadracharyā').[283] Then he should engage himself in the collection of all such accumulations of merit and 'jñāna' like 'dāna' etc. whose core is emptiness and compassion, 'śunyatā' and 'karuṇā.' As has been said in Ārya-dharma-samgiti: "the bodhisattva who sees 'yathā-bhutas' (the reality of things), i.e. emptiness,[284] feels great compassion ('mahākaruṇā') towards beings and he says to himself, 'I must make all beings experience the joy of that samādhi which makes one realise the true state of all phenomena." Goaded by this great compassion, he attains transcendental, true enlightenment ('anuttara samyaka sambodhi'),[285] after fulfilling the three-fold[286] teachings: 'adhiśila,' 'adhichitta' and 'adhiprajñā' teachings: on conduct, teachings on samadhi and teachings on wisdom.

Such is the two-fold-single path of bodhisattvas comprising 'prajñā' and 'upāyaya', which does not sever 'samvriti' or its prop of the apparent even after realising 'paramārtha'. The 'mahākaruṇā' of one who does not cut off 'samvriti' gets engaged in action for beings by becoming 'pūrva-gāmini'[287] (forward leading) without contradictions or contrarities. It has been said in Ārya-ratna-megha: "how does a bodhisattva become proficient in Mahāyāna? Well, in Mahāyāna, the bodhisattva instructs himself in all teachings but does not take to the path of instruction. He does not take to even that what he learns; he does not take to even that which is taught. He does not fall into 'uchheda-driști' (disturbed view) with respect to 'hetu'[288] (cause), 'pratyaya'[289] (factor) and 'nidāna'[290] (links of causation)." It is said in Ārya-dharma-samgiti: "What is the 'pratipatti' (perception, attainment) of a bodhisattva? Now, whatever way the bodhisattvas act through body, speech and mind, they do so with reference to the 'sattvas,' because 'mahākaruṇā' leads ('purvangamā')[291] and they are under the command of 'mahā-karunā' born of the aim of giving joy to all beings." A person with such a beneficial aim thinks: "I have to realise that 'pratipatti' which is beneficial to and confers joy on all 'sattvas'." He possesses the perception of looking at 'skandhas' as illusion but does not wish to give up 'skandhas'. He possesses the perception of looking at 'dhātus' as serpent venom but does not wish to give up 'dhātus'. He possesses the perception of looking at 'āyatanas'[292] as empty entities but does not wish to give up 'āyatanas. He has the perception of looking at forms as the manes of foam but does not give up the realisation or 'sādhana' ('vithapanā') of Tathāgata's 'rūpa-kāyā.[293] He possesses the 'pratipatti' of looking at 'vedanā' as a bubble but it is not the non-emergence of the joy accruing from meditational absorption ('samapatti') of Tathāgata's 'dhyāna' and 'samādhi.' He has the 'pratipatti' of looking at 'samjñā'[294] (consciousness of an object) as a mirage but not as the non-perception of the emergence of Tathāgata's 'jñāna'. He possesses the 'pratipatti' of looking at 'samskāras' as a plantain but not the non-perception of the refinement of Buddha-dharma. He has the realisation of looking at 'vijñāna' as 'māyā' but not the non-perception of the fulfilment ('niṣpatti') of karma through body, speech and mind as its fore-runners." Thus said in detail. The yogi should thus understand from these detailed sūtras the 'pratipatti' comprising 'upāyaya' (means) and 'prajñā' (wisdom).

In this (process), if the practice of 'upāyaya' is not possible during the state of transcendental 'prajñā', but, at the time of practising 'upāyaya', the bodhisattva experiments with transcendental 'jñāna' like a magician unaffected from the true perception (of his work); and after the experiment, he attains wisdom in the form of faith in and knowledge of the 'yathābhuta' (real) aspect of things. This is the very single way (Mārga), comprising the duo of 'prajñā' and 'upāyaya'. The two-fold single path of 'prajñā' and 'upāyaya' as indicated in Arya-akśayamati which says that the (akśaya)[295] state of samādhi, making one aware of these two (i.e. prajñā and upāyaya), should be followed. If the bodhisattva meditates in this manner through the practice of such 'prajñā and upāyaya', for long, he will attain the twelve special states.[296] These very states, with the consolidation of 'guṇas' further and further, establish 'bhūmis'[297] from 'adhimukti-charyā bhumi' to 'Buddha-bhūmi'.[298]

So long as a person does not realise the non-self aspect of all dharmas he is in the 'driḍhtara adhimukti'[299] stage only. When, impregnable to 'māra'[300] etc., the reality ('tattva') is contemplated upon with the force of 'adhimukti' (devotion, faith) then, through the means of the firm 'adhimukti' stage ('bhumi'), the conduct ('charyā') for 'adhimukti' is established. Ārya-ratna-megha describes how, even as a common person, a bodhisattva can become equipped in this 'bhumi' with several qualities like 'samādhi', 'dhāraṇi',[301] 'vimokśa',[302] 'abhijñā'[303] etc. after crossing all adversities of ignorance.

Now, with the four-fold state comprising 'mridu',[304] 'madhya',[305] 'adhimātra'[306] and 'adhimātratā',[307] the four faculties capable of piercing truths are attained. When a little of the sphere of 'jñāna' becomes clear after the apparent connotation (of things) is removed, the probing faculty, ('nirvedha-bhāgiya')[308] called 'ūṣmgata'[309] is born. It is termed as 'the samādhi' which has attained light' (āloka-labdha') in Mahāyāna. When that very sphere of enlightenment ('jñāna-loka') becomes clear in a medium way, it is called 'mūrdhana[310] nirvedha-bhāgiya'; it is also called 'enhanced-light samādhi' ('vridhāloka samādhi').[311] When that sphere of light becomes clearer and is not reflected in the external meaning of things, it becomes 'kśānti-nirvedhiya'[312] owing to the presence still of 'vijñāna'; it is also termed as 'eka-deśa-praviṣta samādhi,[313] because the yogi enters the state of the non-attainment of the 'grāhya' (the object). When the non-dual ('advya'), 'jñāna', born of (the concept of) 'grāhya' and 'grāhaka', the object and the holder, shines forth, it is called 'agradharma nirvedha vāhini';[314] it is also called 'ānantarya samādhi',[315] because the essence of things ('tattva') is entered into after it. Thus far is the 'adhimukti charyā bhumi'.

Other 'bhumis' are established, in brief, as complete with eleven 'angas'.[316] Here, the first 'bhumi' is established after the attainment of the essence of the non-self aspect of 'pudgala' and 'dharmas'. So, when, after the 'agra-dharmas',[317] an absolutely clear knowledge realising the insubstantiality of all 'dharmas' dawns as supra-mundane jñāna, shorn of all deceit, the true realisation of the bodhisattva, having entered the faultless or immaculate state and having generated the 'darśana-mārga,[318] enters the first 'bhumi'. Therefore it is that in this 'bhumi', the bodhisattva feels joy ('pramuditā') owing to his realisation of the unknown 'tattva' or essence for the first tme. Hence, this stage is called 'pramuditā'.[319] One and twelve repugnant-to-sight 'kleśas' are destroyed during this 'bhumi'.

Other 'bhumis' are, in consonance with the 'bhāvana mārga', the path of meditational contemplation. The sixteen 'kleśas' born of three 'dhātus' and which are repugnant to 'bhāvanā' are destroyed in them. Herein 'dāna-pāramitā' or the Perfection of giving is more predominant owing to the bodhisattva's tendency towards others' welfare like his own and his awareness of the arising[320] of 'dharmadhātu'.[321] However, even after knowing the essence of 'bodhi', the bodhisattva stays in the first 'bhumi' so long as he is unable to roam in 'recollectedness' ('samprajñaya') during his deviations from subtle meditation. When he is able to do so, he enters the second[322] 'bhumi' with all its 'angas'[323] complete. Therefore, during this stage, 'śila-pāramitā' is more predominent owing to 'a-samudāchāra'[324] born of deviation from subtle meditation. This 'bhumi' is called 'vimala' as it is shorn of all the taints of unhealthy conduct.

He (i.e.) the practitioner roams about amid the recollectedness of the deviations from subtle meditation. So long as he is not capable of amalgamating all worldly meditations and owning the meaning of all that he has heard, he stays in the second 'bhumi'. When he is capable, he is established in the third stage, all his components ('angas') completed. 'Kśānti-pāramitā' or the Perfection of Forbearance is predominent in this 'bhumi' owing to the bodhisattva's tolerance of all sufferings for the sake of 'practising'[325] what he has heard (from scriptures and instructors) and the accumulation of all worldly meditations. This stage is called 'prabhākari', because it brings about unlimited transcendental knowledge as a beneficial result of these 'samādhis'.

He remains in the third stage in spite of attaining all worldly absorptions so long as he is not capable of roaming about frequently with his already achieved 'dharmas' conducive to the bodhi path and of equanimity in the mind with respect to all kinds of 'dharmas' and absorptions. When he becomes capable of it, he enters the fourth 'bhumi', all his 'angas' completed. In this stage 'veerya-pāramitā' or the Perfection of valour is predominent because of his roaming in the midst of bodhi-inducing 'dharmas' and his constantly correct overpowering of the frivolities[326] of body, speech and mind. This stage is called 'archiṣmati' because of its capacity to burn away the fuel of 'kleśas' and generate the light of bodhi-inducing 'dharmas'. He roams constantly amid bodhi-inducing dharmas. He stays in the fourth stage. So long as he is incapable of turning his mind away from the world and towards 'nirvāṇa' by meditating on the 'satyas'[327] and on the assiduously accumulated bodhi introducing 'dharma', he stays in the fourth 'bhumi'. When he becomes capable of it, he is established in the fifth stage, all his components ('angas') having been completed. This (stage) is called 'sudurjayā', accumulated after a lot of effort, is won with great difficulty.

'Dhyāna-pāramitā' or the Perfection of meditation becomes predominent in this stage by contemplation again and again on the ākāra' or the (constituent) form of the four ārya-satyas' and he (i.e. the bodhisattva) becomes a frequent wanderer in the assiduously collected 'bodhi' path. He is in the fifth 'bhumi' so long as he is unable to enter the absorption of 'a-nimitta',[328] roaming through the creations of a 'nirvatsaka'[329] mind in order to enter 'samsāra' through analysis. When he is capable of it, he enters the sixth 'bhumi', all his 'angas' having been completed. This stage has the preponderance of 'prajñā-pāramitā' or the Perfection of wisdom owing to the bodhisattva's wandering in 'pratitya-samutpād. Because of the pre-ponderance of 'prajñā-pāramitā', he becomes prone towards all Buddha-dharmas. Hence it is called 'abhimukti'.

He becomes the possesser of 'animitta-vihāra'.[330] He stays in the sixth stage as long as he is not capable of attaining the absorption of unblemished roaming in the 'animitta'. When he is able to, he is established in the seventh stage, all his 'angas' having been completed. In this stage, the bodhisattva pierces all 'nimittas' (intentions) with 'animitta' (non-intention) but does not forbid behaviours born of 'nimitta'. So, there is a pre-dominence of 'upāyaya-pāramitā' or the Perfection of means (effort) in this stage. Being connected with the 'anābhoga mārga' or the path of total absorption and hence extremely inaccessible, the stage is called 'durangamā' (reaching afar).

He revels in the unblemished and the 'nirnimitta' (i.e. a stage wherein no causal dharmas affect). He remains in the seventh stage so long as he is incapable of attaining the absorption of the 'anābhoga-vāhi-nirnimitta' stage (i.e. a state of total satiety involving no causal dharmas). When he is able to, he enters the eighth stage, that 'anga' or com-ponent having been fulfilled. This 'bhumi' has the preponderance of Aspirational Perfection (prānidhāna pāramitā) owing to the union of the beneficial aspect (kuśala pakśa) with satiety ('anābhoga'). This stage is called 'achalā' owing to its stability through 'animitta bhoga' (enjoyment based on no nimitta, i.e. immaculate joy).

He becomes a rambler in 'anābhoga animitta'. So long as he is incapable of submitting to do all types of 'dharma deśanā'[331] based on the differences of components[332] and derivations[333] etc. it is still his eighth stage. When he is able to, that 'anga' having been completed, he is established in the ninth stage. That stage has a preponderance of 'bala-pāramitā' or the Perfection of power owing to the bodhi-sattva being equipped with special powers of wisdom with the special force of insight.[334] Being proficient in all types of dharma instruction and possessing the benefit of a special, unblemished intellect, this 'bhumi' is called 'sādhumati'.

In this (stage) he (i.e. the bodhisattva) becomes a beneficiary of the attainment of four experiences ('prati-samvidas'). He stays in the ninth 'bhumi' so long as he is incapable of showing 'buddha kśetra',[335] 'parshata,[336] 'nirmāṇa'[337] etc. and practising total 'dharma' sambhoga' and 'sattva-paripāka'.[338] When he is able to, he is established in the tenth 'bhumi', this 'anga' having been completed. Here the bodhisattva's 'jñāna-pāramitā' or the Perfection of knowledge is pre-ponderant owing to his being equipped with special knowledge for practising 'sattva-paripāka' or the being's well-being. This (stage) is called 'dharma-megha' as it rains a rain of exclusive 'dharma' on innumerable 'loka-dhātus'.[339] These stages are attained by other methods also like 'skandha-pariśuddhi'.[340] These are not being mentioned here for fear of the book becoming voluminous.

Even after attaining 'nirmāṇa-vaśitā'[341] etc., so long as the power to generate enlightenment of all hues of 'asakta'[342] (unattached) and 'apratihata'[343] (invulnerable) types about known phenomena is not born, it still is the tenth 'bhumi'. When he is able to, he enters 'Buddha-bhumi', this 'anga' having been completed. This order of 'bhumis' has been given in Ārya-sandhi-nirmochana. There is no stage higher than this 'Buddha-bhumi' and no other 'bhumi' beyond it has been propounded, because all forms of perfection reach their apex in this 'bhumi'. Even the Buddhas cannot fully describe the virtues of this Buddha-bhumi as they are of immeasurable variety. How can, then, persons like me?

Even 'svayambhu Buddha'[344] cannot, while examining, reach the ends of one virtue (of Buddha-bhumi'). Buddha-dharmas are inexplicable. Only this can be said in brief that Lord Buddha, reaching the utmost bounds of personal and others' acquisitions, residing in the faith of removing all faults, working through his 'sambhoga-kāyā'[345] and 'nirmāṇa-kāyā'[346] in the 'anābhoga' form, by staying in his 'dharma-kāyā',[347] ministering to the well-being of the whole world, will roam the world as long as it lasts. Therefore, wise people should generate faith in the lords who are the treasures of virtue. They should try to practise those virtues in every manner. The virtues of the three bodies ('tri-kāya') etc. are not being stated here lest the book should become voluminous.

May the world with little 'jñāna' soon attain supreme intelligence from the little merit ('punya') that I (may) have earned by describing this path of the 'jina-putras' in accordance with sūtras and 'naya' (the path). This synopsis of 'bhāvanā-krama' has been done by Kamalaśila on the command of King Devarāja.

End of *Bhāvanākrama-I*

BHĀVANĀKRAMA - II

Salutations to Manjuśri Kumārabhuta.[1]

For those entering the path of Mahāyanā, 'bhāvanā-krama' is being stated here in brief. Persons desirous of attaining 'sarvajñatā'[2] as early as possible must endeavour to practise 'hetus' (causes) and 'pratyayas' (factors) which help achieve it. 'Sarvajñatā' is not possible without 'hetu'[3] otherwise it would become attainable by everyone. There can be no obstruction[4] in the feeling of detachment[5] as all do not become 'sarvajña'. Hence, everything depends on 'hetu', because anything may happen to anyone at any time. 'Sarvajñatā' too is possible only for someone some-what somewhere. It does not occur at all times, nor at all places, nor to everybody. Therefore, it is bound to be invariably based on 'hetus' and 'pratyayas'. Of those causes and factors, only those which are 'abhrānta'[6] and 'avikala'[7] should be practised. If one practises 'bhrānta' or equivocal 'hetus', there will be no achieving the desired result even after a long time like (the effort of) drawing milk from horns. There is no generation of fruit or result also without practising all the 'hetus', because there is no possibility of any sprouting in the absence of any seeds etc. Therefore, one who desires that fruit must practise all the 'hetu-pratyayas'[8] or causal factors which are 'abhrānta'.

What are the 'hetu-pratyayas' for attaining the fruit of 'sarvajñatā'? It may be said that a born-blind like me is incapable of revealing them; even then, I shall reproduce from the words of the Lord only who, after attaining supreme enlightenment, uttered them for the benefit of (his) disciples.[9] The Lord had said to them: 'O Guhyādhipati (the lord of 'guhas')! that 'jñāna' of 'sarvajñatā' has compassion ('karuṇā') as its root, bodhichitta as its 'hetu' and 'upāyaya' (practice or effort) as its end (pariavasāna)'.[10] Hence, those desirous of attaining 'sarvajñatā' should get educated in these three: compassion, bodhi-mind and effort.

Inspired by compassion, the bodhisattvas will certainly

undertake the vow to ameliorate the lot of all sentient beings. Then, giving up selfish thoughts, they respectfully engage themselves in the collection of extremely difficult 'jñāna' and 'punyas' through a ceaseless and long period of 'sādhanā'. Entering that 'sādhanā', they are bound to realise that accumulation of 'punya' and 'jñāna' collections. When 'sambhāras'[11] are completed, 'sarvajñatā' will be in hand. Therefore, compassion being the root of 'sarvajñatā', it should be meditated upon from the very beginning as has been said in Ārya Dharma-samgiti: "O Sir! the bodhisattvas should not seek instruction in many dharmas. Sir, if a bodhisattva adopts and realises one single dharma, all (other) Buddha-dharmas will be in the palm of his hand. What is that one dharma? It is 'mahākaruṇā' or great compassion."

Owing to their acceptance of 'mahākaruṇā', the Buddhas stay on till the end of even the world ('sattva-dhātu')[12] inspite of their having attained all the wealth (of 'punya') for themselves. They do not even enter the supremely peaceful city (of 'nirvāṇa') as does a 'śrāvaka'. On seeing sentient beings (in the midst of their sufferings) and because of their abandoning that peaceful nirvāṇa mansion like a lac house ('ayogriha')[13] in flames, the lords' 'hetu' for their unaccepted nirvāṇa is that very 'mahā-karuṇā' alone.

Now, the sequence of meditation on compassion has to be stated, starting with the first inclination ('pravritti').[14] Equanimity (of mind) must first be practised by removing attachment and hatred for all beings with the contemplation of unconcern ('upeksā').

All beings desire happiness; they do not desire 'dukha'. In the endless rounds of 'samśāra',[15] there is no being who has not been related to one a hundred times. So believing, who could be very special to me? (That is, there is no distinction between one being and another). Then, for whom can there be attachment and for whom hatred? Hence, I must have an attitude of equal-mindedness towards all beings. By so contemplating and with a feeling of even-mindedness (madhyastha-bhāva),[16] I should practise equanimity of mind towards friend and foe (alike). After that love ('maitri') should be practised on realising equal-mindedness towards 'sattvas'. If the seed of compassion ('karuṇā') is sown after irrigating the tendencies of the mind with the water of 'maitri' and turning it into a golden piece of earth, the seed will sprout with great felicity ('saralatā').[17] When the procreations or tendencies of the mind[18] get saturated with love, 'karuṇā' should be meditated upon.

This 'karuṇā' (compassion) is of the form of the desire to abolish all 'dukhas' of all beings. All sentient beings of the three worlds are greatly suffering from the triple[19] dukha; so compassion should be meditated upon for all 'sattvas'. Now, those who live as hell-beings are constantly long-submerged in such 'dukhas' as heat (i.e. fires) etc. This has been stated by the Lord. Similarly, the 'pretas' (hungry ghosts), their bodies emaciated with the dukha-fire of extreme hunger and thirst etc.), are described as experiencing extreme suffering. Even the beasts are seen experiencing many kinds of 'dukhas' like mutual devouring, anger, killings and violence etc. Even human beings are seen experiencing immeasurable sufferings from their penury,[20] from search for sensual pleasure, treachery, hurt,[21] separation from loved ones, association with un-loved ones and poverty etc.

Those whose minds are enveloped in various defilements like attachment ('rāga') etc. and those who are drowned in many a deep deviation[22] are all seated on a precipice ('prapāta')[23] owing to the causes of 'dukha' (suffering) and are really very miserable. Even the gods suffer from the dukha of all kinds of 'vipariṇāma'[24] or change (on ripening of the fruit of action). How can the gods who roam about in the realm[25] of desires be happy with their minds always baffled by the grief of the fear of a fall and degradation (from their present status). Sufferings born of mental constituents, which are the cause of defilements generated by 'karma', are of dependent nature and comprise of moment by moment transcience are pervading the whole world. Therefore, seeing the entire world engulfed by the flames of the fire of 'dukha' and thinking 'just as I do not relish dukha so don't others and as to how these dear ones of mine (i.e. the 'sattvas') could be released from 'dukha' and so equating their sufferings with one's own, 'karuṇā' of the type which may be instrumental in removing their sufferings should be meditated upon whether in the 'samādhi' state or during all other 'charyās' (conduct).

Keeping in mind the aforesaid 'dukha' experiences, 'karuṇā bhāvanā' should, first of all, be practised on friends. Then, seeing no distinctions owing to the equality of all beings and by thinking 'all beings are my friends', one should meditate on the middle path ('madhyapakśa').[26] When 'karuṇā' is directed towards all beings as towards one's friends, one should meditate on it for all the beings in the ten directions.[27] When, like the mother of a beloved suffering child, 'karuṇā' of the form of the desire to uplift the beloved one from his suffering, flowing spontaneously, is equitably directed towards all 'sattvas', it is regarded as complete ('niṣpanna')[28] and is designated as 'great compassion' ('mahākaruṇā).

So, first of all, the contemplation of love towards friends is of the form of the desire for attaining joy. Step by step, it should equally be done even for ordinary people as also for one's enemies. By so practising this 'karuṇā', the desire to ameliorate the suffering of all sentient beings will be automatically generated.

Thus, after meditating on root-'karuṇā' or basic compassion, one should meditate on 'bodhichitta'. This 'bodhichitta' is of two kinds: apparent ('samvrita') and ultimate ('paramārtha'). Herein 'samvrita' comprises the undertaking of the vow to work for the welfare of all beings through compassion: 'May I become a Buddha for the good of the world' — this is the first generation of the mind ('chittotpād')[29] of the form of the desire for transcendental enlightenment ('anuttar samyaka-sambodhi').[30] This generation of the mind should be practised by the 'bodhisattva' through another learned scholar established in the vow ('samvara')[31] of 'śilśuddhi' (piety of conduct) and detachment etc. in accordance with the method indicated in 'śila-parivarta'.[32]

After generating 'samvrita' bodhichitta he (i.e. the bodhisattva) should make efforts to generate 'paramārtha' bodhichitta. It has access to the ultimate meaning, is stainless and stable and still like the flame of a lamp in windless calm. Its realisation would be possible through meditation on the union of 'śamatha' and 'vipaśyanā' constantly over a long period coupled with reverence. As has been said in Ārya Sandhi-nirmochana: "O Maitreya! whatever worldly and other-worldly beneficent dharmas of the 'śrāvakas' the 'bodhisattvas' and the 'Tathāgatas', — all are the fruit of 'śamatha' and 'vipaśyanā', because these two are the repositories of all samādhis' as was stated by the Lord in Ārya Sandhi-nirmochana itself: "Whatever the various samādhis' of 'śrāvakas', 'bodhisattvas' and 'Tathāgatas' have been indicated by me should always be regarded as attainable through 'śamatha' and 'vipaśyanā'."

There can be no removal of 'āvaraṇa' or the delusive cover for the yogis by contemplation on 'śamatha' alone; it can merely be a suppression of 'kleśas' or defilements. There can be no real destruction of 'anuśaya'[33] nor its removal without the light of 'prajñā' (wisdom). As has been stated in Ārya Sandhi-nirmochana: "kleśas' are suppressed with 'dhyāna', with 'prajñā' is destroyed 'anuśaya'. 'Ārya Samādhirāja-sūtra' also says: 'howsoever much this 'samādhi' be contemplated upon, it will not destroy self-consciousness ('ātma-samjñā'). It will again incite 'kleśas' as in the case of Udraka's[34] 'samādhi-bhāvanā''. However, if one observes the non-self nature ('nairātmya') of dharmas and, so observing, contemplates, it will become the cause of the achievement of 'nirvāṇa' fruit. Nothing else spells for peace (śānti).

Bodhisattva-pitaka also says: "Those who have not heard this dharma meaning[35] of Bodhisattva-pitaka, being ignorant of the noble Vinaya[36] dharmas and remain content with mere samādhi have a fall through the vanity of the ego and will not be released from birth, old age, disease, death, grief, pain, suffering, ill-will and anger; they will not be released from the six-state round (of 'samsāra'), will not be freed from dukha heaps.[37]" Keeping this in view, the Lord has said: "He who listens to the 'anukūla'[38] (beneficial) from another will be released from old age and death." Hence, a person desirous of generating immaculate knowledge must, after removing all 'āvarṇas', meditate on 'prajñā' by staying in a state of mental equipoise ('śamatha'). Ārya-ratna-kūta also says: "Establishment in 'śila' leads to 'samādhi'; attainment of 'samādhi' will lead to 'prajñā'; unadulterated 'jñāna' bestows the wealth of 'śila'."

It is said in Ārya Mahāyāna-śradhā-bhāvanā sūtra: "O Kulaputra! I shall not speak of as to how, in the absence 'prajñā,' the bodhisattvas' mahāyāna faith will be born in Mahāyāna. O Kulaputra! even with this 'paryāya' or equivalence, whatever mahāyāna faith in Mahāyāna is born in the bodhisattvas, it should be regarded as born of a reflection over the true meaning of dharmas with a staid mind."

The yogi's mind will become distracted by sense objects if insight ('vipaśyanā') is not accompanied by calm ('śamatha') or equipoise; it will remain unstable like a lamp in the midst of wind. The glow of 'jñāna' will not be very clear. So, both (i.e. 'śamatha' and vipaśynā)' should be equally practised. It has been said in Ārya Mahāparinirvāṇa-sūtra "The 'śrāvakas are unable to see Tathāgata's 'gotra' owing to excess of 'samādhi' and paucity of 'prajñā'. The bodhisattva can see (Tathāgata's 'gotra'), but not clearly owing to excess of 'prajñā' and paucity of 'samādhi'. The Tathāgata is all-seeing owing to an equal measure of 'śamatha' and 'vipaśyanā'." Owing to the power of mental equipoise ('śamatha') the mind does not waver even in contrary winds like a lamp unaffected by the wind. With insight ('vipaśyanā') it becomes invincible for others owing to the removal of profanities of a deviated sight. As has been said in Ārya Chandra-pradeepa-sūtra: "The power of 'śamatha' makes one un-wavering; the power of 'vipaśyanā' makes one mountain-like." Hence, the union of both these has been ordained.

In the first instance, the yogi, in order to realise 'śamatha' and 'vipaśyanā' should quickly and straight-forwardly practise the collections of 'śamatha' (equanimity) and 'vipaśyanā' (insight). Now, what is 'śamatha sambhāra' (equanimity accumulation). It comprises residence in a conducive place, desirelessness, contentment, the renouncing of many an act, purification of conduct and the giving up of the contradictory desires etc. A conducive place is that which has five qualities: 'sulabdha' (well-got) owing to the availability of food and clothing etc. without much difficulty; 'susthāna' (good spot) owing to the absence of evil persons and enemies etc.; 'subhumi' (good land) owing to its being a land without disease etc.; 'sanmitra' (friendly, owing to its being tolerant ('sama-dristi') like the conduct ('śila') of a friend; 'suyukta' (appropriate) owing to its being not too crowded with people during day and of little noise at night. What is meant by desirelessness or little desire? (It means) having little attachment or desire for one's 'cheevara'[39] to be either fine or in access (of requirement). What is contentment? To remain satisfied with the possession of ordinary 'cheevara' (cloth) or wrapping gown. What is meant by giving up many actions? It is the giving up of such evil acts as buying and selling, of too much dialogue between the householder and the renunciate; forsaking praise and the making of medicines and the calculation of stars etc.

What is the purification of 'śila'? The non-discontinuation of right instruction during both 'samvaras' (vows) whether in 'prakriti'[40] (deviation) or 'pratikśepa'[41] (contradiction); and if it is discontinued through negligence, it has to be diverted towards the pursuit of dharma through repentance.

Whatever has been said in 'śrāvaka' vows[42] about the (preventive) precautions[43] for a 'pārājika'[44] is inappropriate. Even then, repentence is imperative after which one must resolve mentally not to repeat it but to observe or experience 'nissvabhāvatā' through the very mind which inspired one to do that act and this would lead to the purification of 'śila' too. This can be learnt from Ārya Ajāta-śatru-kaukritya-vinodin.

Therefore, after removing the faulty act ('kaukritya'), one should practise meditation ('bhāvanā').

Even in (the realm of) desires, various faults accruing from them here and hereafter (i.e. in next life) should be mentalised and their contrarities should be given up. All feelings of 'samsāra', whether pleasant or unpleasant are fleeting, destructible. Undoubtedly, there is bound to be separation between them and me; so why should I be excessively attached to them? Thinking in this manner, all 'vikalpas' must be eradicated.

What is meant by 'vipaśyanā-sambhāra' or accumulation of insight? (It consists of) refuge in the good people, search for the 'bahuśruta' or the reputed scholars and mentalisation of 'yoniśa' ('samādhi'). What kind of a good person should be sought for refuge? One who is well-versed (well-reputed), frank of speech, compassionate and capable of enduring 'dukha'. Now, what is the meaning of 'search for the 'bahuśruta' (it is the search for) one who listens very reverently to the 'neyārtha' (dubious interpretation) and the 'neetārtha (intelligible interpretation) of the Lord's twelve-point[45] dharma discourse. It has been said in Ārya Sandhi-nirmochana: "not to listen to the noble discourse as one may desire is a hurdle in 'vipaśyanā'." It again says: "Vipaśyanā' is born of the clear vision generated by listening and reflection." Ārya Nārāyana-pariprichhā also says: "Prajñā dawns on him who listens; the one with 'prajñā' has his 'kleśas' calmed."

What is 'yoniśa mansikāra'? For a bodhisattva who has to decide correctly about the intelligible sūtras[46] and the equivocal sūtra[47] meanings to become rid of all doubts is to become single-mindedly assured in meditation (bhāvanā). Otherwise, seated in the wavering vehicle of doubt, he will not attain single-minded decisiveness anywhere like a person in the midst of a road junction ('śringātaka').[48]

The yogi should always abstain from meat and fish etc. and take only limited, conducive food. Thus should a bodhisattva, who has accumulated all the collections of 'śamatha' and 'vipaśyanā', enter meditation ('bhāvanā').

Now, at the time of practising 'bhāvanā', the yogi should, first of all, finish up his routine acts, be done with toilet etc. Without a jarring tone and seated at a mentally convenient place, thinking "I have to establish all beings in the bodhi-adorned ('bodhi-manda)[49] state', keeping in view 'mahā-karuṇā' which aims at the well-being of the whole world, bowing to all the Buddhas and bodhisattvas in all the ten directions with his five limbs, fixing in front or on some stool the image or the picture of Lord Buddha and the bodhisattvas in accordance with liking (or mental inclination) worshipping and eulogising them, repenting of one's sins and commending the world's 'punyas', sitting in 'semi-paryanka' or full 'paryanka'[50] posture of Bhattārka Vairochana[51] in an extremely easy pose,[52] eyes neither too open nor too closed, fixing the gaze on the tip of the nose, nor bending the body too much nor keeping it too erect, keeping the body at ease, turning recollectedness inwards, the bodhisattva should make himself seated. Thereafter, he should keep both his shoulders upright. The head, neither too upraised nor too bent, should be fixed motionless to one side; the nose should be straight navel-ward. The lips and the teeth should be gently placed and the tongue should touch the roots of the upper teeth. Inhaling and exhaling should neither be too loud nor thick ('sthūla') nor too vast but the breath go in and come out slowly with automatic ease ('anābhoga').

Here, first of all, 'śamatha' has to be realised. After quietening the disturbing contrarities of the mind from external objects, bringing it back constantly inwards towards the 'ālambana', the establishment of contentment ('prīti')[53] and peace ('prasrabdhi') in the mind, these spell out 'śam-atha'. Contemplation over the ultimate nature of things by holding on to the prop of 'samatha' is called 'vipaśyanā'. As has been said in Ārya Ratna-megha: "The concentration of mind is 'śamatha' and the insight into things is 'vipaśyanā'."

Arya Sandhi-nirmochana also says: "Lord! how can the realisation of 'sāmatha' and proficiency in 'vipaśyanā' be achieved?' 'O Maitreya! it is said that there is a dharma cure or method established by me. It is like this: whatever sūtras, 'geya',[54] 'vyākaraṇa'[55] 'gāthā'[56] 'undāna',[57] 'nidāna',[58] 'avadāna',[59] 'iti-vrittaka',[60] 'jātaka',[61] 'vaipulya',[62] 'adbhuta dharma'[63] and 'upadeśa-varga'[64] have been told by me to the bodhisattvas, after carefully listening to those, owning them up properly, practising (their) recitation, analysing them well through the mind, piercing with insight (lit. vision), sitting in solitude at a lonely place, completely absorbed inwardly, one should mentalise such dharmas as one deems proper, because the very mind which mentalises also reflects in it that mentalisation through constant contemplation. Thus entering it and staying in it for many a time, whatever bodily calm ('kāya-prasrabdhi')[65] or mental calm ('chitta prasrabdhi') is attained, that in itself is called 'śamatha'. Therefore, the bodhisattva looks for 'śamatha'. It leads to bodily peace and mental peace. After achieving them, he stays in them and, removing the confusion of the mind, he sees during 'śamatha' the reflection of those very dharmas which have been contemplated upon; develops faith. The reflection seen during 'śamatha' is analysed for the state of its deeper or inner meaning ('jñeyārtha'). Thorough analysis, correct concept, observation, zeal, desire (to know), noticing the fine nuances (of analysed dharmas), understanding and absorption, all these consitute 'vipaśyanā' and are called the skills ('kauśala') of a bodhisattva's insight or 'vipaśyanā'.

The yogi desirous of the accumulation of 'śamatha' should first fix his mind on the accumulation of such things as 'sūtra varga' or sūtra compendiums, singable sūtra portions etc. and their entire discourses ('pravachana'), inclination toward 'tathatā' ('tathata-parāyaṇa'), descending into 'tathatā' ('tathatā prāga-bhāram') and march 'tathatā-ward'. Then, he should fix his mind in the 'skandhas' of all the different types of many dharmas together or he should fix his mind on that image of lord Buddha as heard of or seen by him. As is stated in Ārya Samādhirāja; "The lokanāthas' (lords of the world) are resplendent on all sides with bodies of golden hue. He whose mind is established in this 'ālambana' that bodhisattva is of an equanimous mind ('samāhita')."

In this manner, the mind should be fixed on the very prop ('ālambana') he (i.e. the yogi) wishes to and, afterwards, he should do it increasingly. Having fixed the mind on it (i.e. the prop), the mind should be tested in this way; 'does it properly hold on to the 'ālambana' or does it get absorbed or gets baffled owing to disturbance ('vyāseka')[66] from external objects?' Thus should it be examined. If overcome by indolence ('styāna') and cowardice ('middha'), the mind becomes absorbed or shows signs of getting absorbed, he should at once conceptualise mentally the supremely joyous things like the image of lord Buddha or an awareness of light ('alöka-samjñā'). Then, calming down absorption ('laya') he should act in a manner that the mind's 'ālambana' should become very clearly reflected into that 'ālambana' itself.

When like one blind from birth or like a person in dark or like one with eyes shut, one cannot see the 'ālambana' (mental prop) clearly, it should be regarded as absorbed ('leena'). When running about external forms and their supposed qualities etc. or through other mentalisations or, through a previously experienced thing, there arises insolence ('audhitya') and it is feared it may perk up in the mind also, at such times, the yogi should mentally contemplate on the transitoriness of all 'samskāras' or on 'dukha' itself, — things which grieve the mind. Then, after calming down all contrarities, the mind's elephant should again be tethered to the same 'ālmabana'-pillar with the rope of recollectedness ('smriti') and awareness ('sam-prajñayā'). When absorption and insolence disappear and the mind looks to be calmly installed in that 'ālambana', then, suspending satiety ('ābhoga'), one should stay in that state with detachment for as long as one wishes. Thus the practitioner practising ('śamatha'), achieving bodily and mental peace, when capable of steadying his mind on the 'ālambana' as he desires, should regard 'śamatha' as having been realised by him.

After realising 'śamatha', one should meditate on

'vipaśyanā'. One must think like this; 'all the words of lord Buddha are beautiful utterances ('subhāṣita'), because they, either manifestly or by tradition, express the ultimate meaning or essence ('tattva') or lead towards it.' When the essence of things is discovered, one will be freed from all the meshes of view or sight ('driśti-jāla') just as darkness disappears at the dawn of light. 'Śamatha' alone will neither purify 'jñāna' nor dispel the darkness of super-imposition ('āvaraṇas'); 'jñāna' is purified by proper meditation ('bhāvanā') on the 'tattva' with 'prajñā' (wisdom). The 'tattva' is reached through 'prajñā' only. 'Prajñā' alone removes superimposition ('āvaraṇa') properly. Hence one should think; 'I must search for 'tattva' with 'prajñā' after establishing myself in 'śamatha'; I should not be contented with 'śamatha' alone'.

What is the essence ('tattva') like? It is that which, in the ultimate sense, is void of any self in all things and 'pudgala dharmas?[67] It can be reached through the perfection of wisdom ('prajñā-pāramitā') and in no other manner. As has been said in Ārya Sandhi-nirmochana; "Lord! by which perfection ('pāramitā') is the 'nissvabhāvatā' of all dharmas attainable by the bodhisattvas? 'O Avalokitesvara! it is attainable through 'prajñā-pāramitā' (the perfection of wisdom). Therefore, staying in 'śamatha', one should meditate on 'prajñā'?"

Here, the yogi should deliberate like this: 'pudgala', is not seen seperate from 'skandha' (heaps), 'dhātu' (elements) and 'āyatana'(entrances). However, 'pudgala' is not of the nature of 'skandhas' etc., because the latter are impermanent and of varying nature while, as some believe, 'pudgala' is permanent and of one (unvarying) nature. In reality, for the indescribable 'pudgala' to be a 'thing' is improper because of the absence of any other types of 'vastu-state' (permanent entity or an existing thing). Hence, it must be considered that to utter 'I' and 'mine' (for any supposed thing or entity) in the world is mere delusion.

The non-self nature of all 'dharmas' should be similarly

meditated upon. Briefly speaking, 'dharmas' comprise the five skandhas,[68] the twelve 'āyatanas'[69] and the eighteen 'dhātus'.[70] Here, those that are with form, such as 'skandhas', 'dhatus' and 'āyatanas' are not different from the form of the mind in the ultimate sense, because there is an absolute absence of the certainty of self-nature ('svabhāva') when they are divided into atoms and even when sub-atoms are analysed. Therefore, owing to a superimposition of false forms etc. since time immemorial the ignorant persons see their mind alone as over-casting external forms like the emergence of forms in a dream. 'In the ultimate sense ('paramārtha') these forms etc. are not different from the forms of the mind,' — this is how one should ponder over. Thus, the seeker should regard the 'tri-dhātu' as mind alone. So concluding the mind to be manifesting all dharmas and analysing them, he realises the nature of all dharmas and of the mind too. Thus, does the yogi reflect.

Even for the mind to be true in the ultimate sense is inappropriate. Where can the truth about the mind which, after assuming the forms of false appearances, appear in varying forms. Just as forms are false so is the mind which is not apart from them. Just as forms etc. being of different kinds are neither of one nor of several natures, similarly the mind, being not apart from them, is neither of one nor of several natures. Therefore, mind is of the nature of illusion (māyā) only.

Just as the mind is so are all dharmas too of the nature of 'māyā', this should be reflected upon. When the nature of the mind is so analysed by the seeker through 'prajñā', the mind, in the ultimate sense, is not found either inside or outside nor in both; neither the past mind is found nor the future nor the present mind. When generated, it comes from nowhere nor goes anywhere on cessation, because the mind is not graspable, is undirected and is without form. As has been said in Ārya Ratna-kūta; "O Kaśyapa! the mind is untraceable even when reached. That which is untraceable cannot become an 'ālambana'; that which can not be made an 'ālambana' has neither a past nor a future nor a present." Thus on examination, one does not see the beginning, does not see the middle, does not see the end of the mind.

Just as the mind is without an end or a middle so should one understand all dharmas to be without an end, without a middle. Thus knowing the mind to be without end or middle, one does not discover any self-nature of the mind as such. That which analyses the mind appears all to be empty ('śunya'). On knowing the latter, the nature of the appearance[71] in the mind and the nature of forms etc. will also not be correctly seen. Thus, when the nature of all 'dharmas'[72] is not correctly observed through 'prajñā', whether form is transient or permanent, void or non-void, unclean or clean,[73] created or uncreated, existent or non-existent, he (i.e. the seeker) does not think of such 'vikalpas' or alternatives. Just as he does not find a 'vikalpa' for form ('rūpa'), so also he does not entertain a 'vikalpa' for 'vedanā,'[74] 'samjñā',[75] 'samskāra',[76] and 'vijñāna';[77] When the existence of dharmas cannot be substantiated, its qualifying attributes also cannot be proved to exist. So, how can there be a 'vikalpa'(for something which is non-existent)? In this manner, when the yogi does grasp the conclusion about the ultimate nature of things after an analysis through 'prajñā', he enters 'nirvikalpa samādhi' and also comes to realise the non-substantiality ('nissvabhāvatā') of all dharmas.

He who after analysing the nature of things through 'prajñā' does not meditate on it but only meditates on forsaking[78] mentalization is never freed from 'vikalpas' and will also not realise 'nissvabhāvatā' owing to the absence of the glow of 'prajñā'. So the lord has said that through right analysis and with the fire of the correct knowledge of things, the yogi will burn the tree of the fictional mind[79] like the churning of fire by the 'arani'.[80]

Ārya Ratnamegha says; "Thus he who is skilled in washing away faults, in order to remove all frauds for contemplating 'śunyatā' (he) practises yoga. His awareness of 'śunyatā' enhanced, wherever his mind roams, in whatsoever his mind busies itself, he realises on analysis all those things to be void or empty by nature. The mind itself, when analysed, appears empty ('śunya'). The mind which analyses also appears to be 'śunya' of any self-nature on examination. Thus examining, he (i.e. the yogi) attains 'animitta yoga'.[81] This indicates the entry into the 'nirnimittatā'[82] stage through the lead or guidance of analysis.

It has been clearly indicated how it is absolutely impossible to enter the immaculate ('nirvikalpa') state by merely giving up mentalisation ('mansikārita') without reflecting on the nature of things through 'prajñā' or wisdom. So the yogi after thoroughly and correctly examining the nature of forms etc. through 'prajñā' and not by confining himself in forms sits in meditation. He does not practise 'dhyāna' by staying in the middle of this world and the next owing to the non-availability of those forms etc. Hence, this is called 'unfixed meditation'.[83] When he enters 'anupalambha dhyāna,'[84] after analysing all things through 'prajñā' it is called 'prajñottara dhyāna' or post-wisdom meditation as has been indicated in Ārya Gaganaganja and Ratna-chūḍa.

He having realised the reality of the non-self nature of beings ('pudgala-dharma nairātmya'), being beyond the need for the observation or analysis of any other thing owing to its non-existence, devoid of the din of argument and counter-argument, of his own volition and with natural ease should meditate on the reality ('tattva') clearly and stay in it. Staying there, he should not disturb mental emanations ('chitta santāna'). In between, if the mind is disturbed from the outside by attachment ('rāga') etc., knowing it to be a deviation and quickly quietening down the mind from reflection over the harmful (deviation) he should once again make the mind enter 'tathatā'. If he finds the mind uninterested therein, he should reflect over the benefits of 'samādhi' and mentalise interest in it. Disinterestedness in seeing the faults of (his) deviation ('vikśepa') should also be calmed down. If there is an apprehension of the mind relapsing into absorption ('laya') owing to a dim instigation[85] from indolence and cowardice, it must be quickly calmed down by mentalising an extremely joyous object as mentioned earlier and the same 'tattva' should be firmly held as a support. If on a recollection of some previous light-heartedness the mind tends to become flippant, one must mentalise, as already stated, the fleeting aspect of painful things and calm down the mind. After that the mind should again be attuned to the same 'tattva' through an approach[86] of natural ease or felicity.

When detached from 'laya' and 'audhatya', the mind gets clearly attuned to that essence ('tattva') of its own volition, the 'sādhaka' or seeker should practise detachment ('upekśā') by de-activising effort ('bhoga');[87] if 'ābhoga'[88] (multiplicity) is indulged in when the mind is properly attuned ('sampravritta'), it will become confounded. On the mind being even absorbed, if 'ābhoga' is not practised, it remains bereft of 'vipaśyaṇā' owing to excessive stupor or absorption. Therefore, when the mind is in a state of 'laya' effort must be done (to stir it out of its state) but 'bhoga' should not be done in the attuned state. When 'vipaśyanā' is contemplated upon, prajñā becomes heightened; then, owing to the paucity of 'śamatha', the reality is not clearly seen due to the wavering of the mind like a lamp in the wind. So 'śamatha'(calm) must be meditated upon at that time. When 'śamatha' gets excessive, 'prajñā' (wisdom) should be meditated upon.

When both (i.e. calm and insight) attain a balance, one should stay in that state through 'anabhisamskāra' or an attitude of effortless repose as long as the body and the mind do not feel an ache. During the interval of this body-mind ache, look at the whole world as 'māyā' (illusion), a 'marich' (mirage), a dream-snare, a mere moon-in-water reflection and then reflect like this: 'these 'dharmas' have become complicated in the world as there is no knowledge of true or serious ('gambhira') dharma; hence, I shall so act as to make (the beings) aware of true 'dharmatā' or the reality of things'. So reflecting, one should place 'mahā-karuṇā' and 'bodhicitta' in front. Then, after a little respite, he should again enter 'the state of meditation wherein all dharmas are unfelt ('sarva-dharam-nirābhasa samādhi'). He should again relax when the mind becomes over-wrought. This is the duo-leading ('yuganaddha-vāhi') path of 'śamatha' and 'vipaśyanā', which depends on the prop of 'savikalpa' and 'nirvikalpa' reflections, that is, admixed and immaculate perceptions.

In this manner, the yogi should continue to remain seated, meditating on 'tattva' for an hour, a half 'prahara', a full 'prahara'[89] or for as long a period as he may desire. The 'artha-pravichaya dhyāna' or the meditation which leads to sifting the true meaning of the things has been indicated in the Ārya Lankāvatāra. After this, rising up from 'samādhi' but without undoing the lotus pose, he (i.e. the yogi) should reflect 'all these dharmas, although non-existing in the ultimate sense, are stationed in apparent phenomena ('samvriti'); otherwise, how could the fruit of action ('karma-phala') relationship be established? 'The lord too had said; 'things are created in 'samvriti' but they are non-existent in 'paramārtha' (ultimate sense).'

One must ponder like this; 'ignorant people super-impose existence over non-existent things. In this manner their intellect gets baffled and for long do they wander in the rounds of 'samsāra'. Therefore, after completing supreme 'punyas' and 'jñāna' accumulations and attaining the 'sarvajñatā' state, I shall educate those people about the truth of the things ('dharmatā').' After this, the yogi should slowly undo his lotus posture and make obeisance to all the Buddhas and bodhisattvas in the ten directions and, after worshipping and eulogising them, he should undertake the great vow ('mahā-praṇidhāna') of 'ārya-bhadracharyā'.[90] After that an effort should be made to accumulate all endless 'punyas' and 'jñāna' collection replete with emptiness ('śunyatā') and supreme compassion ('mahākaruṇā').

Such 'dhyāna' is free from all kinds of superimpositions. As has been stated in Ārya Ratna-chuḍa; "wearing the armour of love ('maitri') seated on the throne of great compassion ('mahākaruṇā'), he pracitses the 'dhyāna' of the accumulation ('abhinirhāra') of the emptiness of all superimpositions ('sarvakāra-varopeta 'śunyatā'); what is that 'emptiness of all superimpositions? (It is that) detailed as non-deviation ('anapagati')[91] from 'dāna', non-deviation from śila, non-deviation from 'kśānti', non-deviation from 'veerya', non-deviation from 'dhyāna', non-deviation from 'prajñā', non-deviation from 'upāya' etc." Thus in detail. The bodhisattva should work for the maturation of sattvas' (punya) or 'sattva-paripāka'[92] and must practise such 'kuśalas' (beneficient means) like 'dāna' (giving) etc. which generate such wealth as field (kśetra), body (kāyā) and proliferation (bahu-parivāra) etc.

In the absence of the above, whose would be the fruit of that wealth called 'Buddha kśetras' (field)? So 'sarva-kāravaropeta' is that knowledge or that 'sarvajñatā', which, being full of such efforts as 'dāna' etc. has been defined by the lord as the one 'with the proficiency of efforts attained'. Therefore, not 'śunyatā' alone but the methods (upāyaya) of 'dāna' etc. should also be practised by the boddhisattva. Ārya Sarva-dharma Vaipulya says; "O maitreya! this method advocates the coming together of Six Perfections for the boddhisattvas' enlightenment. The ignorant people may comment that the boddhisattva may be educated in 'prajñā-pāramitā' alone and that there is no need of other perfections (for him). Well, such people tarnish other 'pāramitās' (per-fections) too. So, what do you think, O Ajita! Was Kaśirāja[93] a fool to give away his own flesh in lieu of that of the pigeon? "No Lord!" replied Maitreya. The lord continued, "O Maitreya! whatever 'kuśala mulas'[94] or root merits com-prising the Six Perfections were accumulated by me while practising the conduct of a bodhisattva, did they prove harmful for me?" "No, Lord!" replied Maitreya. The lord said, "you also properly practised 'dāna-pārmitā' for sixty aeons (kalpas), 'śila-pārmitā' for sixty aeons, 'kśānti-pārmitā' for sixty aeons, 'veerya-pārmitā' for sixty aeons and 'prajñā-pārmitā' for sixty aeons. Even then the ignorant people will say that a single path ('naya') like 'śunyatā' can lead to 'bodhi'. Such people will become impure of conduct."

The bodhisattva, with wisdom alone and without efforts and means, cannot execute Lord Buddha's work like a 'śrāvaka' cannot (execute). With the help of means ('upāyaya') only will he be able to do so. As has been said in Ārya Ratnakuta; "O Kaśyapa! just as kings execute their job with the assistance of a minister, so also the bodhisattvas' 'prajñā', coupled with the skill of 'upāyaya', executes all Buddha works." The direction of the bodhisattvas' path is different; that of the 'tirthikas'[95] and of 'śrāvakas' is different. The direction of the 'tirthikas' path, owing to its contradictions of self ('ātma') etc. is totally shorn of 'prajñā' (wisdom); so there will be no attainment of release ('mokśa') for them.

The 'śrāvaka' stage being devoid of 'mahākaruṇā' does not consist of 'upāyaya'; so they tend to devote themselves to (the persuit of) solitary nirvāṇa. The bodhisattva path is regarded as comprising 'prajñā' and 'upāyaya'. So they become inclined towards un-installed or un-calculated nirvāṇa. The bodhisattva path being that of 'prajñā' and 'upāyaya' they attain un-fixed or un-installed (apratiṣthita) nirvāṇa. He does not fall into the 'samsāra' because of the force of 'prajñā' and does not fall into (the 'srāvaka's calculated) nirvāṇa due to the force of 'upāyaya'.

Ārya Mārga-śirṣa says, "these two, in brief, are the paths of bodhisattvas. What two? 'prajñā' and 'upāyaya!" Arya Śriparamādya also says, 'Prajñā-Pāramitā', is the mother and skilful means (upāyaya), the father." Also (said) in Ārya Vimalakirti-nirdeśa-sūtra; "What fetters a bodhisattva, what his release? Holding on to the round of 'samsāra' without 'upāyaya' is the bodhisattva's fetters, the crossing of the samsāric round with 'upāyaya' is his release. Holding on to the round of 'samsāra' without 'prajñā' is his fetters; crossing the round with 'prajñā' is his release 'Prajñā' (wisdom) not attached to 'upāyaya', (means) is fetters; 'prajñā' attached to 'upāyaya' is release. 'Upāyaya' unheld by 'prajñā' is fetters; 'Upāyaya' held on to by 'prajñā' is release". Thus (said) in detail.

If the bodhisattva practises 'prajñā' (wisdom) alone, he will fall into the 'śrāvaka's' desired 'nirvāṇa' and so into ties ('bandhana'); 'apratiṣthita nirvāṇa' will not give release. Thus 'prajñā' without 'upāyaya' becomes a bondage for a bodhisattva. Therefore, like people plagued by wind (humour) using heat, or fire, the bodhisattva should practise emptiness through 'prajñā' coupled with 'upāyaya' in order to counter the wind of contradiction ('viparyāsa'); he should not get to it (i.e. 'śrāvaka's nirvāṇa in actuality or manifestly ('sākśāta') like a 'śrāvaka'). As is stated in Ārya Daśa-dharma-sūtra; "O Kulputra! just as a person serves fire and reveres it, treats it (respectfully) like his own preceptor but still thinks that that fire, so worshipped, respected and revered by him, cannot be held by him in both his hands. Why? Because he knows that by so doing he will get physical pain and mental worry. Similary, the bodhisattva does not manifestly take to 'nirvāṇa' although aspiring after it. Why so? Because he believes that by accepting 'nirvāṇa' he would retreat from enlightenment ('bodhi')."

By practising 'upāyaya' alone the bodhisattva, having not crossed a common man's stage, will remain totally bound. Hence, 'upāyaya' should be practised along with 'prajñā'. Like poison overcome by mantra-efficacy, the 'kleśas' of a bodhisattva too turn into nector by meditation through the power of the adoption of 'prajñā'. What, then, to speak of 'dāna' etc., which by their very nature, bear beneficient fruit. It is said in Ārya Ratnakūta; "O Kaśyapa, just as poison accompanied by 'mantra' and medicine does not kill so also the bodhisattvas owned by 'prajñā' do not have a downfall through their 'kleśas'."

The reason due to which the bodhisattva does not give up the world is the power of his 'upāyaya'; because of that (very reason) itself he does not fall into the 'śrāvaka's nirvāṇa. The reason due to which he removes all props ('ālambana') is the power of 'prajñā'; because of that very reason itself, he does not fall into 'samsāra'. So he attains the Buddhahood of un-established nirvāṇa. It has been said in Ārya-gagana-ganja;

"All 'kleśas' are stopped by that 'prajñā jnāña' and all sattvas are not forsaken owing to 'upāyaya Jñāna'?" Ārya Sandhinirmochana also states; "I have not spoken of supreme or transcendental enlighten-ment ('anuttara samyakasambodhi') for those who totally remove themselves away from the sattvas' service or well-being, nor for those who totally turn away from the refinement ('abhisamskāra') of their 'samskāras'. Hence, he who is aspiring after Buddhahood should practise both 'upāyaya' and 'prajñā'."

At the time of meditating on transcendental wisdom or at the time of the extremely exalted state ('samāhita'), when it is not possible to practise 'upāyaya' like 'dāna' etc., whatever 'prajñā' is there as part of the experiment ('prayoga')[96] and partial attainment ('priṣtalabdha'),[97] that itself constitutes the practice of 'upāyaya'. Hence both wisdom and means occur simultaneously and that, in fact is the single duo-path of 'prajñā' and 'upāyaya' of the bodhisattvas. Owing to their being equipped with 'mahā-karuṇā', which looks over all the sentient beings, they pursue or practise the transcendental path and, at the time of ameliorative effort or means (utthānopāyaya) also, like a magicican, practise uninterrupted 'dāna' etc. As has been said in Ārya Akśyamatinirdeśa; "And, what is the bodhisattva's 'upāyaya'? What is accumulation of prajñā? It is that exalted absorption by which the mind gets fixed on the 'ālambana' (support) of 'mahākaruṇā'(great compassion) by looking at 'sattvas'; it is 'upāyaya'. That which gives the exalted absorption of peace and supreme peace is his (i.e. the bodhisattva's) wisdom or 'prajñā'?" Māradamana-parichheda also says ; "Moreover, the elevating practice of the bodhisattvas is linked with the knowledge of 'prajñā'; with the knowledge of 'upāyaya' it unites itself with the accumulation of beneficient dharmas. With wisdom knowledge it engages itself in 'nairātmya' (non-soul) 'asattva' (non-being), 'ajiva'(non-self), 'apoṣa'[98] (non-permanence), 'a-pudgala'[99] (non-existence of 'pudgala'). With 'upāyaya' jñāna, he is to be engaged in the proper maturation ('paripāka') of all sentinent beings." Ārya

Dharma-samgiti-sūtra also says; "just as a magician, ready to undo (the magical object of) his creation, has no attachment towards it as he is aware of its reality, so also the bodhisattvas wear an armour for the world, considering all the three states of existence to be illusory and thus become proficient in 'sambodhi' (enlightenment)". It is said that the way of the bodhisattvas comprising 'prajñā' and 'upāyaya' can be employed even when staying in the midst of the world by keeping the goal in view; it can also be used while staying in desired or fixed nirvāṇa ('āśaya-nirvāṇa').[100]

After practising such 'upāyayas' (means) as giving ('dāna') etc. which have transformed themselves into supreme 'sambodhi' comprising 'śunyatā' and 'mahākaruṇā', (the bodhisattva) should, regularly meditate on 'śamatha' (calm) and 'vispaśyanā (insight) as much as possible for the sake of generating 'paramārtha bodhicitta'. Arya gochar-pariśuddhi-sūtra says; "skill in means should always be meditated upon through current recollectedness as instructed in the same manner as the constant eulogisation of bodhisattvas who are ever engaged in the good of sentient beings."

He who meditates on 'karuṇā', 'upāyaya' and 'bodhicitta'—compassion, means and bodhi-mind in the above manner certainly becomes distinguished in this life. He will have the 'darśana' (sight) of Buddha and the bodhisattvas in dream; he will also have other good dreams. Gods will protect him through (their) commendation. Every moment will spell for massive accumulation of merit and knowledge. Stains of defilements will be destroyed; joy and amiability will always increase. He will become the darling of the many. The body also will not contract any ailment. The alacrity of the supreme mind will be attained and special qualities like detachment or unconcern ('abhijñatā') will accrue.

After this the yogi, by the power of 'riddhi'[101] (special attainments), goes to various 'loka-dhātus' (world) and worships the Buddhas; he also hears dharma from them.

He will surely have the holy sight of the Buddhas and the bodhisattvas at the time of his death. In the next birth also, he will be born in a distinguished place and family, haloed by Buddhas and boddhisattvas. In this manner he will, without much ado, complete his merit ('punya') and 'jñāna' collections. He will become the great enjoyer (of bliss) and have a large family (of spiritual aspirants). He will also help many persons with his incisive insight. He will remember all his births in every birth. One must also learn about similarly laudable and high praise (for this path) mentioned in other sūtras.

In this manner, meditating on 'karuṇā', 'upāyaya' and 'bodhicitta' reverently, for long, 'paramārtha bodhichitta', accumulated through 'darśana mārga' is born through the generation of the extremely pure moment in the tendencies of the mind and their consequent maturation as also meditation on the essence of things up to its last limit like the churning fire with 'yajña' fuel, the decline of contrarities due to supreme knowledge, an absolutely transparent dawning of 'dharma-dhātu' devoid of 'prapaneh' (falsehood), absolute staidness like the unflickering lamp in a neat, quiet and windless state or place, and full realisation of the 'tattva' with its non-self nature. When such 'bodhichitta' is born, one enters the 'ālambana' upto the totality of things. He is born into Tathāgata's 'gotra' (class) and becomes inclined towards unblemished conduct and indifferent towards all worldly tendencies, is established in a state of the awareness of 'dharma-dhātu' and 'dharma-dhātu' of the bodhisattvas and attains the first stage ('bhumi'). This kind of praise of 'bodhichitta' can be learnt in detail from daśa-bhumiśvara[102] etc. This 'dhyāna' which provides the 'ālmbana' of 'tathatā' is indicated in Ārya lankāvatāra. This leads to the unsullied state of the bodhisattva's immaculate 'samādhi'.

The inclination towards 'adhimukti bhumi' is possible through 'adhimukti' (faith or 'śraddhā') and not through (mental) refinement ('abhisamskāra'). When that knowledge dawns, he directly enters (the 'bhumi'). After entering the first 'bhumi' (stage) in this manner, he attains the 'ālambana' of 'proficiency in performance' (kārya-niṣpatti)[103] in the path of meditation (bhāvanā) through the contemplation of 'prajñā' and 'upāyaya' with the help of transcendental ('lokottara') and later accumulated ('priṣtalabdha')[104] 'jñāna' by purifying one after the other, the lower 'bhumis' in order to achieve better and better attributes ('guṇas') with the cleansing[105] of accumulated dross (of 'āvarañа') which (only) 'bhāvanā' can destroy; the yogi thus enters the bounds of 'Tathāgata's' boundless jñāna and the ocean of 'sarvajñatā. This sequence of purification of the tendencies of the mind has been mentioned in Ārya Avalokiteśvara. This leads to the purely immaculate state of the bodhisattva. As has been said in Ārya Sandhi-nirmochana also; "(The bodhisattva) will become enlightened with the boundless transcendental knowledge."

Owing to his having entered the ocean of 'sarvajñatā' he, like the wish-fulfilling gem, possesses sustenance factors or 'guṇa' heaps for all the sattvas as sanctified by the fruits of earlier vows, having attained the habit of supreme compassion, equipped with many 'upāyayas' through 'anābhoga' (non-concernment), the fulfiller of all the purpose of the entire world through endless ways, having attained the ultimate limit of the highest attributes, wanderer in the boundless world of 'sattvas' after eliminating the dirt of all the faults of lust; so seeing the seer, after generating faith in lord Buddha, the treasure of all 'guṇas' (excellent attributes), should himself make all efforts to achieve the perfect fulfillment of those qualities. So the lord has said, "This 'sarvajña jñāna' (the knowledge of the ultimate reality of things) has compassion as its root, 'bodhichitta as its cause and 'upāyaya' as its fulfullment or consummation". With their stains of jealousy etc. removed, the noble persons remain unsatiated with (the accumulation of) attributes or qualities like oceans with water. They accept beneficial words after examining them just as the swans royal gladly separate milk from water.(1)

Hence wise persons should put aside the mind baffled by prejudices and accept good words even from the ignorant.(20)

The merit that I have earned by thus speaking of the

Mādhaymika way, may it help all people to attain the mahayāna path.

The middle part of Bhāvanākrama written by Acharya Kamalaśila ends.

This version has been settled after the translation done by the Indian Pandita Prajnavarmana and Lotswa (the translator) Reverend Jñānasena.

End of *Bhāvanākrama-II*

BHĀVANĀKRAMA - III

'Bhāvanākrama' or 'the sequence of meditation' is being described here in brief for those who have entered the path in accordance with the way of Mahāyāna sūtras. Therein, although the lord has taught about the different 'samādhis' of the buddhisattvas as 'aparimita'[1] and 'apramāṇa'[2] even then 'śamatha' and 'vipaśyanā' include all samādhis. That is why it is called the duo-path of equipoise and insight. The lord has said, "By meditating on 'śamatha' and 'vipaśyanā' a person gets released from the bondage of wickedness[3] and of nimitta.[4]" Therefore, those desirous of removing all superimpositions ('āvarṇas') should practise 'śamatha' and 'vipaśyanā'. The mind becomes motionless like a lamp in a windless place, through the force of 'śamatha'. Through 'vipaśyanā' is generated the glow of the true knowledge due to the revelation of the real nature of 'dharma tattva'. Then the entire 'āvaraṇa' is removed like the (disappearance of) darkness with the light of dawn.

The lord, therefore, has ordained four things for the yogis: 'ālambana'; 'nirvikalpa pratibimbakama'[5] (directly perceived reflection) 'savikalpa pratibimbakama'[6] (mentally acquired reflection), 'vastu-paryantatā'[7] (the ultimate limit of things) and 'kārya pariniṣpatti'[8] (fulfilment of work). Whatever 'ālambana' is practised through the reflection of all dharmas and the devotion or faith ('adhimukti') in Buddha images etc. along with 'śamatha' is called 'nirvikalpa pratibimba'. It is 'nirvikalpa' or immaculate because it analyses the true meaning of all phenomena in an absolute ('avikalpa')[9] manner. It is a reflection ('pratibimba') because it comprises meditating on the reflection of all see-able and acceptable 'dharmas' as 'ālambana'. When the yogi, in order to understand the meaning of 'tattva' deliberates on that very reflection through 'vipaśyanā', it is called 'savikalpa pratibimaba' owing to the generation of analytical option ('tattva-nirupaṇa vikalpa')[10] indicating 'vipaśyanā'. Analysing the nature of that very reflection, the yogi learns the nature of all 'dharmas' like one surely coming to know of all the deformities of his face by seeing the reflection in a mirror. When he realises the such-ness (tathatā) of the quality of the end of all things then, owing to the attainment of all total limits of things ('vastu-paryantatava'),[11] it is called 'vastu paryanta[12] ālambana' in the first 'bhumi'. After that, like using the elixir[13] of a medicine, through the mode of meditation (bhāvanā), due to the generation of a genuine interest in other bhumis respectively and with the attainment of 'āśraya pravritti',[14] when the yogi achieves the 'kārya samāpatti'[15] of the total removal of all superimpositions, that very 'jñāna' is termed as 'kārya niṣpatti ālambana' or 'the prop of all fulfilment of action' in 'Buddha-bhumi' (the stage of boddhisattvahood).

Now what does all this prove? (it shows that) the limit or end of all things is realised through meditation on 'śamatha' and 'vipaśyanā', which leads to the all-āvaraṇa-removing absorption in the objective, that is, the achieving of 'bodhi'. Therefore, he who aspires to attain 'buddhatva' should practise 'śamatha' and 'vipaśyanā'. He who does not practise these two attains neither 'vastu-paryantatā' nor 'kārya niṣpatti'; 'śamatha' here is the concentration of the mind and 'vipaśyanā' the examination of phenomena ('bhutas').

The lord has breifly spoken of the qualities of 'śamatha' and 'vipaśyanā' in Ārya Ratna-megha etc. Here, the yogi, through staying in the accumulation of 'śamatha' and 'vipaśyanā' by purifying 'śila' etc. and by generating great compassion for all sentient beings, should practise hearing[16] dharma, reflecting[17] over it and meditating by means of the awakened 'bodhichitta'.

At the time of 'bhāvanā' (meditation) the yogi should first of all complete his routine duties like toilet etc., sit at a convivial place where no jarring noise disturbs and, undertaking the vows: 'all beings have to be established in the glory of 'bodhi' by me', keeping in view 'mahākaruṇā' which aims at the well-being of the entire world, bowing with his five limbs to all Buddhas and bodhisattvas in the ten directions, installing the (image and pictures of) Buddhas and bodhisatttvas on a stool or elsewhere, worshipping, praising them as he may wish, confessing his own sins and commending the virtues of the whole world, seating himself on a gentle seat in the 'paryanka' posture of Bhattāraka Vairochana, or in the half 'paryanka' posture with eyes neither too shut nor too open and gaze fixed on the tip of the nose, the body erect but at ease and neither too stooping nor too stiff, should make his 'smriti'[18] or recollectedness inward-looking. Then the shoulders should remain level, the head neither raised nor bent but staying steady on one side. The nose should be in line with the navel and the tongue should touch the root of the upper teeth. Incoming and outgoing breath should neither be loud nor gruffy nor fast but automatic and natural with measured inhalation and exhalation.

The yogi should first of all practise 'śamatha' by concentrating his mind on that image of Tathāgata which he has seen or heard of. Then, decorated with such special marks as shine like heated or burnt gold, sitting in the midst of the Buddha family (parsana-maṇḍala)[19] and ministering in myriads of ways to the welfare of beings, by constantly mentalising such an image of Tathāgata, the yogi should generate an aspiration for (the cultivation of) Tathāgata's (guṇas) (qualities or attributes). After calming down absorption, insolence etc. he should continue meditating till he sees (during 'dhyāna') Tathāgata as vividly as the image in front of him. Then, he should contemplate on 'vipaśyanā' by observing the reflection of Tathāgata's image as it appears, disappears and appears (again and again). After that he should deliberate like this; 'just as the reflection of Tathāgata's image neither appeared from anywhere nor will disappear anywhere and the seated image is also without any self-entity ('svabhāva') and devoid of 'self' and I-ness, similarly all 'dharmas' are devoid of (true) existence, (devoid of self and devoid of I-ness); they neither come (from anywhere) nor go (anywhere) and are without an entity like the reflection'. So deliberating and meditating on the tattva (reality) with an immaculate and an indescribably composed mind, he should continue to be seated as long as he wishes. This 'samādhi' has been indicated or designated as Ready-Buddha-Seated-in-front 'samādhi'. Its detailed 'anuśamsā' (commendation) should be studied in the sutra of that name.

In such ways comes about 'dharma' acquisitions (dharma samgraha). By fixing the mind on these, one must practise 'śamatha' for the calming down of absorption (of attachment) and insolence. In fact, all dharma acquisitions are vis-à-vis 'rūpa-arūpi-bheda'[20] (the distinction between the form and the formless). Those acquired from 'rūpa-skandha'[21] are called 'rūpi' (with form); those acquired from 'skandhas' (heaps) of 'vedanā' (feeling)[22] etc. are called 'arūpa' (without form). The ignorant people owing to their fixation in the acquisition of 'bhāva' (worldly things) etc. wander in the 'samsāra' with their intellects deluded. The 'yogi', in order to remove their delusion and by directing his 'mahākaruṇā' towards them should meditate on 'vipaśyanā' (after perfecting 'śamatha'), in order to realise the 'tattva'. The examination of 'bhutas', (things or phenomena) is called 'vispaśyanā' and 'bhuta' in turn, is 'pudgala' and 'dharma-nairātmya' (non-self, non-existent).

Now 'pudgala nairātmaya', is the non-self and non-I-ness of 'skandhas' and 'dharma-nairātyma' is the delusion thereof. The yogi must examine this. There is no 'pudgala' separate from 'rūpa' or form etc. owing to its non-reflection (apratibhāsa)[23] and the factors like 'I am' are born from form (rūpa) etc. only; nor is 'pudgala' of the nature of 'rūpa-skandhas' (form-heaps) etc. because form etc. are transitory and various by nature and 'pudgala' has been imagined by some as permanent and of one form. It is not appropriate for 'pudgala' to be thing ('vastu') owing to its being indefinable from the point of view of 'tattva' and its separate-ness ('anyatva') and (also) because reality ('vastu-sata')[24] has no other form. Therefore, for people to speak of 'I' or 'mine' is merely a foolish delusion. Then, he should, in order to attain 'dharma nairātmya', consider whether these 'form dharmas' are permanent entities seperate from the mind or that it is the mind itself which is reflected in form ('rūpa') etc. like forms in a dream. Examining them in their atoms or sub-atomic parts, he will discover nothing. Thus, not finding anything, he becomes bereft of the contradictions of being and non-being, is-ness and is-not-ness.

The mind manifests the three 'dhātus' too, as is said in Lankāvatāra; "Matter can be divided into atoms but 'rūpa' (form) should not create contradictions in form. Those with damaged sight cannot understand the play of the mind".

The yogi reflects like this: "It is the mind alone which, since time immemorial, appears externally as different forms etc. to the ignorant owing to its wrong fixation on false forms etc., like appearances in a dream. Therefore, concluding the mind to be the manifestation of all dharmas and analysing them, he comes to understand the nature of all phenomena and examines the mind. He deliberates like this; "The mind is also uncreated, like an illusion, in the ultimate sense. When the mind itself appears in various forms after assuming illusory shapes of 'rūpa' etc., how can then its own existence be established, owing to its not being different from (those) forms etc. The mind, when being created, comes from nowhere and goes nowhere during cessation. It is uncreated by itself, by others or by either of these in the ultimate sense. Hence, the mind is like an illusion (māyā). Just as the mind is, so are all 'dharmas' illusory, uncreated in the ultimate (paramārtha) sense."

The nature of mind by which the yogi examines (phenomena) is also not traceable on examination. So to whatever 'ālambana' the yogi's mind travels, its nature or substantial is-ness is not traced on examination. When that is not found, understand all things to be without a real basis like the mass of a plantain stem. The mind, then recedes. In this manner, having become shorn of the contradictions of 'bhāva'[25] etc. and the old illusion[26] gone, he attains 'nirnimitta yoga'.[27] Thus Ārya Ratnamegha says, " In this way he (i.e. the yogi), proficient in washing the dirt of (all) faults, attains yoga through meditation on 'śunyatā' for the removal of all 'prapancha' or illusory falsities."

His 'śunyatā' meditation thus augmented, to wheresoever his mind travels or to whatsoever he engages it, he realises the emptiness of those places (and things) after searching analysis. The mind itself, on examination, appears empty by nature. Thus, through close examination, he enters 'nirnimitta yoga'. He also comes to know that he who does not examine (things) closely, cannot enter into the 'nirnimitta stage'.

Examining the nature of 'dharmas' in this manner, when he does not find anything, he neither postulates 'there is' nor 'there is not'. He who regards it as 'not there'; receives no reflection in his 'buddhi' (intellect). If 'bhāva' is noticed sometimes, he should imagine its presence as 'not there'. If the yogi, examining with his wisdom, does not discover any 'bhāvas' during the three 'kāla's (times) (i.e the past, the present, the future), what postulates shall he imagine as being 'there is not'? So, in that situation, he has no other alternatives owing to the preponderance of 'bhāva' (is-ness) and 'abhāva' (is-not-ness) over all alternatives ('vikalpas'). When there is no 'pervading thing' (vyāpaka),[28] there cannot be any 'pervaded object (vyāpya).[29] So the yogi enters the unaldulterated imma-culate stage, and he does not rely on form etc. either. Because of his not finding any substantial existence of things on examination with 'prajñā' he becomes a 'beyond wisdom' ('prajñottara') practitioner. Having thus entered the essence or secret ('tattva') of the non-self of 'pudgala dharma', due to the absence of anything else worth examining and his mind in its own volition in consequence of such thinking amid the prevailing immaculate-ness ('nirvikalpa rasa'), the yogi should remain seated by holding on to that 'tattva' clearly with no mental exercise. Staying in that state, he should not allow any aberrations of the mind.

If the mind, during the period, gets diverted towards externals, he should examine its nature to calm down the mind and then re-engage it in meditational practice. In case the mind does not appear engaged, he should observe the characteristics of 'samādhi' and contemplate engagement therein. When (the mind is) disturbed, he should observe the (characteristic) faults and overcome disinterestedness. If, with the coming on of lethargy ('styāna') and indolence ('middha'), the mind appears to be apparently absorbed or about to relapse into absorption, he should overcome that 'laya' (absorption inertia) by mentalising such joyous things as the form of lord Buddha and consciousness of light etc. Then hold on firmly onto that 'tattva': if the yogi is unable to hold on to 'tattva' in a clear manner as would not one who is blind from birth or has entered darkness or has closed his eyes, his mind should be regarded as 'leena' (absorbed in inertia) and as devoid of insight ('vipaśyanā'). If he finds the mind uppish in between owing to a (revived) desire for previously experienced objects or there is an apprehension of uppishness ('audhatya'), he should mentally ponder over the painfully fleeting (nature of) things and calm down (that) uppishness. After that, he should again make an effort to effortlessly engage the mind in that very 'tattva'. When, like a battled person or like a monkey, the mind gets distracted, it should be taken as an indication of uppishness and the absence of equipoise or calm ('śamatha'). When retrieved from such obsorption or 'inertia' ('laya') and uppishness, the mind, engaged again of its own volition, re-yoked to that very 'tattva', the yogi should de-activate enjoyment (ābhoga) and practise detachment ('upkeśā'). Then alone should the single-duo path of 'śamatha' and 'vipaśyanā' be considered as perfected.

When meditating on 'vipaśyaṇā' (insight) 'prajñā' becomes excessive owing to the paucity of 'śamatha', the 'tattva' will not be very clearly visible due to the restlessness of the mind like a lamp in the wind. 'śamatha' should be meditated upon at that time. On 'samatha' growing excerssive, 'tattva' will not be very clearly visible to one overwhelmed by indolence. 'Prajñā' should be meditated upon at that time.

When both are equally engaged like two oxen (yoked) to a single yoke, the yogi stays in 'anabhisamskāra' till the body and the mind ache.

Briefly speaking, all 'samādhis' sufffer from six faults; laziness,[30] ālambana – forsaking,[31] inert absorption,[32] uppishness,[33] non-effort,[34] and effort.[35]

As opposed to them, one should contemplate the eight dispelling-samskāras'[36] which are (mental) faith,[37] desire[38] (to act), effort,[39] alacrity or activeness,[40] recollectedness,[41] awareness,[42] consciousness[43] and detachment. Of these the first four are the opposition of laziness, because with faith in efficacious qualities, the yogi's craving (for meditation) is born. Craving leads to effort ('veerya') and when effort starts, the body and the mind become active. With this activeness of the body and the mind laziness, (kausīdya) is removed. Therefore, 'sraddhā' etc. are meant for the removal of laziness, they must be contemplated upon. The prop of recollectedness ('smriti') is the opposite of forsaking or abandoning ('sampramoṣa'). Awareness ('samprajñaya') is the opposite of inert absorption ('laya') and uppishness ('audhatya'), because they are stopped when noted by it (i.e. 'samprajñaya'). If 'laya' and 'audhatya' are not calmed down, 'anābhoga' will accur. As opposite to it (i.e. anābhoga or disaffection), 'chetanā' or consciousness should be meditated upon. When the mind becomes calm after the removal of inertia and uppishness, the fault of satiety ('ābhoga') occurs. As opposed to it, detachment ('upekśa') should be meditated upon.

If 'ābhoga' occurs when the mind is evenly engaged, it (i.e. the mind) gets confused. If 'ābhoga' is not felt when the mind is in 'laya' (inertia), the mind being without 'vispaśyanā' (insight), it will become totally inert ('leena') like a blind person. Therefore, such mind should be controlled, its uppishness curbed and detachment ('upekśa') again be practised in that equanimous state.

After this, the yogi should remain seated in the contemplation of 'tattva' through 'anabhisamskāra' (the last of the four releases) for as long as he wishes. In between, when the body and the mind ache, the yogi should again and again think of the world to be an illusion, a dream, a reflection of the moon (in water). As has been said in Avikalpa-praveśa. "(He) sees all dharmas like the surface of the sky through his transcendental knowledge; with this background, he regards them as 'māyā', a mirage, a dream, a reflection of the moon in water." Thus realising the world to be an illusion and directing his great compassion towards beings, he should think like this: "these ignorant people, unaware of the reality of 'dharmas' superimpose existence on basically non-existing dharmas and becoming baffled, gather many, many 'karmas' and 'kleśas'. Thus they continue to wander in the cyclic round. I will, therefore, so work that I could make these people aware of true 'dharmas'?" After a little rest, the yogi should again engage himself in 'sarva-dharma-nirābhasa samādhi' (the samādhi in which no 'dharmas' exist). In this manner and in this sequence should he (i.e. the yogi) sit (in meditation) for an hour, a half 'prahara' (i.e. about an hour and a half), a full 'prahara' (i.e. about three hours) or for as long as possible.

Now, if he desires to rise up from his 'samādhi', he should diberate over it without undoing the squatting posture ('paryanka') like this: although all these 'dharmas' are uncreated in the ultimate sense but they still appear like 'māyā' in varying and unthinkably attractive forms owing to a certain conglomeration of causal factors ('hetu-pratyaya'); as such, there will be no chance for a refutation ('uchheda driṣti') and no end to contradictions ('upavāda'), because nothing will come to hand on examination through 'prajñā'. Hence, there is neither the context of a permanent view nor any end to superimpositions ('samāropa'). Here, those whose understanding is baffled owing to the confusion of their wisdom-eye, perform a lot of karmas through self-conceit and so go on wandering in the cyclic round. Those who, completely indifferent towards the world, without 'mahākaruṇā', continue to practise the perfection of giving ('dāna') etc. for 'sattvas', descend into the enlightenment of the 'śrāvaka' and the 'pratyeka-buddha' owing to their being devoid of effort ('upāyaya').

Those regarding the world to be without true existence ('nissavabhāva') and vowing to uplift the entire world through the force of 'mahākaruṇā', their intellect being unbaffled as a magician's, fulfil the accumulation of 'punya' and 'jñāna'- collections, attain the Tathāgata status and they will live forever till the end of the world by fulfilling all the joys and welfare of the world. They, due to the force of their 'jñāna'- collections, having removed all 'kleśas' never fall into 'samsāra' nor do they descend into 'nirvāṇa' owing to the accumulations of immense and immeasurable 'punya' through their concern for all beings; such as these become the sustenance of all beings. 'Therefore, I, desirous of the happiness and comfort of all 'sattvas' and aspiring for 'unfixed nirvāṇa' ('apratisthita nirvāṇa'), should always endeavour for immense 'punya' and 'jñāna' collections, thus should he think.' As has been said in Ārya Tathāgata-guhya sutra also; "Jñāna accumulation is for the removal of all defilements ('kleśas'), 'punya'- accumulation is for the sustenance of all 'sattvas'." Therefore, the lord bodhisattva mahāsattva should always endeavour for 'punya-sambhāra' and 'jñāna sambhāra' i.e. accumulation of merit and accumulation of knowledge. Ārya Tathāgatotpatti-sambhava-sūtra also says; "There is only one reason for Tathāgata's rebirth. What is it? O Jinaputra (son of the conqueror)! Tathāgatas are reborn owing to tens of thousands of immeasureable causes. What are those, then? (They are) the causes for the rightful fulfillment of their insatiate accumulations of merit and knowledge." Ārya Vimala-kirti-nirdeśa also states. "The tathāgata's bodies are born of hundreds of merits, of all the meritorious dharmas, and of the countless 'roots of noble dharmas ('kuśal-dharma mūla') etc."

Then, undoing the 'paryanka' posture slowly he should offer obeisance to all the Buddhas and boddhisattvas stationed in the ten directions and, after worshipping and eulogising them, he should perform such vows as 'āryabhadracharyā' etc. After that he should engage in the attainment of all such 'punya' accumulations as 'dāna' etc., which have been dedicated (for the sattvas' well-being) through such supreme enlightenment as is embraced by 'śunyatā' and 'karuṇā'.

Those who believe 'sattvas' under the sway of good and bad 'karma', born of the contrarities of the mind, wander in 'samsāra' after enjoying heaven etc. as the fruit of their actions' and those who think nothing, perform no actions and hope to be released from 'samsāra' without needing to think anything or do any 'kuśala karma' believing that conduct such as 'giving' (dāna) etc. has been indicated for ignorant fools; it is through people of both these categories that entire Mahāyāna gets negated and Mahāyāna being root of all vehicles (yāna), its negation will spell the negation of all other vehicles. The attitude of 'nothing need be thought of' will mean the negation of 'prajñā' (wisdom) which analyses phenomena ('bhutas') as analysis or examination alone is the root of true knowledge ('jñāna'). When that is negated, transcendental wisdom will also be negated owing to the severing of its root. With 'lokottraprajñā' gone, omniscience ('sarva-kārjñatā') will also get negated. To say that beneficient conduct like 'dāna' etc. should not be practised will invariably lead to the negation of 'upāyaya' such as giving ('dāna').

Briefly speaking, 'prajñā' and 'upāyaya' alone constitute Mahāyāna. As Ārya Gayā-śirṣa says; "These two alone are the bodhisattva's way. What two? Well, 'prajñā' (discriminating wisdom) and 'upāyaya' (meaningful effort)." Tathāgata-guhya-sūtra too says, "Prajñā and upāyaya' are meant for the accumulation of all the perfections ('pāramitas') by bodhi-sattvas." Therefore, the denial or negation of Mahāyāna will create a massive 'karma' superimposition ('karmāvaraṇa'). So the wise person desirous of his own good should abandon even from a distance, like poisoned food, such poisonous words as are opposed to scriptures ('āgama') and logic ('yukti') from people who deny Mahāyāna, are of selfish intent, render not service to the learned and imbibe not the spirit of Tathāgata's words and who, as self-destroyers, are also destroying others.

Negation of the analysis of things ('bhuta') will spell the denial of the most prominent of bodhi components, the 'pravichaya' (analysis) of dharmas. In the absence of 'bhuta' examination, with what will the yogi make his mind enter immaculateness ('nirvikalpatā') when the mind has been prone to fixation in such entities as form ('rūpa') etc. since time immemorial? If it is said that all dharmas can be understood without recolleted-ness and without mentalisation, it is not appropriate, because all experienced things ('dharmas') cannot be subjected to non-recollectedness and non-mentalisation without 'bhuta' examination. 'I do not have to recollect these 'dharmas'; I do not have to mentalise them'; if, by thinking in this manner, the contemplation of non-recollectedness and non-mentalisation is practised on those dharmas, they are bound to become recolleted and mentalised. If the mere absence of recolleted-ness and mentalisation is taken for non-recollectedness and non-mentalisation, it has to be thought out as to how the is-not-ness of both can come about. To have a 'hetu' (cause) for 'abhāva'(is-not-ness) is inappropriate. How can immaculation ('nirvikalpatā') ensure from the 'nirnimitta' (non-conceptualised) and the non-mentalised? Even an unconscious person being devoid of recollectedness and mentalisation can also be regarded as being in the 'nirvikalpa' state as a consequence of such stupor ('avikalpatā'). There is no other means except 'bhuta' -examination by which non-recollectedness ('a-smriti') and non-menatalisation ('a-manasikārita') can be brought about.

Undoubtedly, even during 'a-smriti' and 'a-manasikāra' the non-self-existence of 'dharmas' cannot be (fully) realised with 'bhuta' examination (alone). 'Dharmas' are not empty ('śunya') by nature'; now, this kind of a stipulation cannot be pierced through except through an analysis of emptiness. The removal of the 'āvaraṇa' is not possible without the realisation of 'śunyatā'; otherwise, everyone everywhere will be entitled to 'mukti' (liberation).

What of the yogi who does not practise recollectedness ('smriti') and mentalisation ('manasikāra') owing to his giving up the former or out of sheer folly, how can such an extremely foolish person become a yogi? Without examination of things and being engaged in 'a-smriti' and 'a manasikāra', he will become engrossed with delusion alone which will snuff out the light of true knowledge. If he is not shorn of recollectedness nor is he foolish, how will he be able to practise non-recollectedness and non-mentalisation without 'bhuta' examination? It would be appropriate to say that such a person does not recollect while recollecting, does not see while seeing. How, with the practice of non-recollectedness and non-mentalisation, will buddha-dharmas like the previously residual and continued recollectedness ('anusmriti')[44] etc. arise owing to the (inherent) contradiction involved? The experiencing of cold as opposed to heat does not permit the feeling of heat!

If the 'samādhi'-proficient yogi has any psychological knowledge, he must invariably have an 'ālambana'. The common people cannot be suddenly enlightened without an 'ālambana' (prop). By what opposing thing is the superimposition of mental defilements ('kleśas') removed? There is no possiblity for cessation of the mind[45] for the common person who has not attained the Fourth Dhyāna.[46] Therefore, non-recolletedness and non-mentalisation that have been spoken of for a good religious conduct ('saddharma') or true 'dharma' should also be viewed in the context of 'bhuta' examination only and not otherwise. So, when the yogi, examining through correct 'prajñā', does not observe the arising of any 'dharma' in all the three times (i.e. the past, the present and the future), how shall he (be able to) do 'manasikāra' and 'smaraṇa' (mentalisation and recollection)? He who even during the three times, has not experienced the 'asattvas'[47] in the ultimate sense, how may he have recollectedness or mentalisation? For this very reason, he enters the immaculate 'jñāna' in which all contradictions have cessation or are warded off. Entering it, he realises 'śunyatā' and realising it, he removes all snares of deviation.

The practitioner of wisdom ('prajñā') coupled with means ('upāyaya') becomes totally proficient in 'samvriti' (the apparent) and 'paramārtha' (the ultimate) truths. So by attaining knowledge bereft of superimpositions, he attains all 'Buddha-Dharmas'. Therefore, without 'bhuta' analysis, there is neither the dawn of true knowledge nor the removal of 'kleśa' cover. It is said in Manjuśri Vikurvata-sūtra; "O Dārikā![48] how does a bodhisattva become the victor in the battle'? (Reply) 'O Manjuśri! by not coming across any 'dharmas' after repeated examination". Hence the yogi, with his eye of knowledge wide open and after totally overcoming his 'kleśa' foes with the weapon of 'prajñā' wanders about without fear un-like a frightened coward with eyes closed. It is said in Ārya Samādhirāja-sūtra also: "If one examines non-self 'dharmas' and, examining them, meditates, it becomes a cause for the attainment of 'nirvaṇa' fruit; any other cause ('hetu') brings not peace." Sūtra-sammuchaya also says; "Himself engaged in the practice of 'vipaśyanā', if one does not help others engage themselves in 'vipaśyanā', it (i.e. his own practice) becomes an evil act."

'Vipaśyanā' is of the nature of 'bhuta' analysis; this has been stated in Ārya Ratna-megha and Sandhinirmochana etc. Says Ārya Ratnamegha; "The knowledge of the non-true existence of things ('nissvabhāvatā') through analysis with insight ('vipaśyanā') is termed as entering the 'nirnimitta'." Ārya Lankāvatāra also says; "O wise one! the 'bhāvas' when examined by the intellect do not yield any 'jñāna' about their individual and general characteristics. That is why it has been said that all 'dharmas' are non-existent. If 'bhuta'-examination is not done, it will lead to a refutation of the many kinds of analytical methods suggested in the 'sūtras' by the lord. As such it would be proper to say that we, of little intellect and less courage, are incapable of (understanding) erudite ('bahūśruti')[49] analysis. The lord had praised erudition a lot; therefore, it is never appropriate to refute it."

It has been said in Punarbrahma-pariprichhā: "Those who get engaged in thinking over un-thinkable 'dharmas', experience perversion of thought ('ayoniśa').[50] Also, those who imagine as created 'dharmas' which are uncreated in the ultimate sense and regard them as transient and full of suffering as 'śrāvakas' do, get into the 'ayoniśa' (perversion) state owing to their thinking being bereft of (the two factors of) 'samāropa' (superimposition) and 'apavāda' (contradiction)", (that is, because they do not consider the two factors).

Whatever has been said in refutation of such tendencies is not a refutation of (the desirability of) 'bhuta'-analysis which has been recommended by all the 'sūtras'. Brahma-pariprichhā-sūtra itself says; "Chitta-śura (valiant of mind) bodhisattva has said that he who thinks over all dharmas with the mind and remains uncovered and untouched by them is called a 'bodhisattva' as such." Again it says': "How do they (i.e. the bodhisattvas) become valorous? Well, when they do not find the 'sarvajñatā' mind while looking for it, they alone will become wise who examine abstract ('yoniśa'), 'dharmas'; they categorise 'dharmas' as illusion ('māyā') and mirage ('marichi')."

It should be known that whenever the din of words like 'achintya' (unthinkable) etc. is heard, it is meant for propounding the analysis of the core entity ('pratyātma-vedaniyatā') of 'dharmas' for the refutation of the ego of such people as believed in the realisation of the reality ('tattva') only through hearing and deliberating it; it also refutes 'ayoniśa' of the mind (i.e. the mind's adherence to wrong, pervert 'dharmas'). It certainly does not mean a refutation of 'bhuta' examination; otherwise, as already stated, it would mean a contradiction of various arguments ('yukti') and scriptures ('āgama'). Whatever knowledge is gained through 'prajñā' born of hearing and thinking should be contemplated upon through meditational wisdom and nothing else. A horse runs (well) on its familiar race-course, so 'bhuta' examination or 'the analysis of all phenomena' must be practised. Although it may (turn out to) be of an opposite nature but, owing to its being of the quality of correct mentalisation ('yoniśa manasikāra'), it generates undifferentiated ('nirvikalpik') 'jñāna'. With this belief, he who is desirous of such 'jñāna' should practise this (examination of 'bhutas'). Ārya Ratna-kūta says that with the generation of the fire of right 'nirvikalpa jñāna', it will burn itself away in that fire like two faggots burning themselves out in the fire generated by their own rubbing ('gharṣaṇa') together.

It is (sometimes) said that no 'kuśala' (meritorious) acts etc. need be done as the exhaustion of 'karma' leads to liberation. Well, such a belief will (only) lead to 'ājivaka-vāda'.[51] That the exhaustion of 'karma' leads to liberation has not been propounded in the Lord's word. How then? (i.e. how can 'mukti' or release come about)? Well, through the cessation of 'klesas' (mental defilements). It is not possible to exhaust action ('karma') (already) performed since eternity, because they are innumerable. While suffering the fruit of such actions during lower births, more karmas are generated. The non-cessation of 'kleśas' makes them the cause of the non-cessation of 'karma' just as the light of a lamp will not cease without the lamp being put out. It has already been stated that the cessation of 'kleśas' is impossible for one who denies 'vipaśyanā' (insight). If it is agreed that the practice of 'vipaśyanā' is essential for the cessation of 'kleśas', 'kleśa' cessation itself will give liberation and the labour for the exhaustion of 'karma' will become meaningless. To say that non-meritorious (a-kuśala) action should not be performed is appropriate. Why 'kuśal karma' is refuted is that if its performance generates 'samsāra', it is not proper. And, only those 'kuśala' acts are 'samsāra' prone which are born of all the contrarities of 'self' etc. and (certainly) not the actions of boddhisattvas which are born of great compassion ('mahākaruṇā') and their dedication of 'punya' (pariṇamita) through transcendental enlightenment. So it has been indicated about the 'pariṇāmana' (dedication) of these very ten 'kuśala dharmas' as (acts of) extreme purification in the 'sādhana' (practice) of the 'śrāvakas', the 'pratyeka-buddhas', the 'bodhisattvas' and the Buddhas. Ārya Rantnakuta also states; "Like the collection of water from all the great rivers into the great ocean, the root-merits ('kuśala-mula') collected by the bodhisattvas through various means, after being transformed into 'sarvajñatā' become one taste (i.e. equanimity) in (that) omniscence (which reveals the true nature of things)."

The wealth that the Buddhas and the bodhisattvas earn in the shape of (their) physical form ('rūpa-kāyā'), field-purification ('kśetra-pariśuddhi'),[52] aura (prabhā),[53] proliferation ('parivāra'),[54] full happiness ('mahābhoga')[55] etc. is the fruit of the accumulation of 'punya'; so has it been mentioned here and there in the sūtras by the Lord; these too will get negated. The refutation of 'kuśala' conduct also means the refutation of the vow of emancipation ('pratimokśa samvara)[56] etc. Thus his (i.e. the yogi's) shorn head and begging bowl etc. will be of no avail; when 'kuśala' action becomes indifferent to 'purification' ('abhisamskāra') it will lead to indifference towards 'samsāra' and towards actions for the sake of 'sattvas'. In consequence, it will also make 'bodhi' (enlightenment) a distant thing. It has been said in Ārya-sandhi-nirmochana; "I have not spoken of supreme true enlightenment for those who totally turn away from actions for 'sattvas' and from the rectification of 'samskāras." Ārya Upali-pariprichhā also says. "To be indifferent towards 'samsāra' constitutes great misconduct for 'bodhisattvas'. Accepting 'samsāra' is supreme good conduct." Ārya-Vimala-kirti-nirdeśa also states: going into samsāra with 'upāyaya' is release for boddhisattvas. 'Prajñā' without 'upāyaya' is shackling, 'upāyaya' with 'prajñā' is release; 'prajñā' with 'upāyaya' is release." Ārya Gaganaganja says, "To be averse towards 'samsāra' is evil karma for bodhisattvas." Also said in Sūtra-sammuchaya, "Even 'asamskrita dharmas' are to be analysed and to be averse to 'samskrita dharmas' is evil 'karma'." If he knows the 'bodhi'-path but does not investigate the way of Perfections ('pārmita-yāna'), it is tantamount to doing 'māra-karma' (evil 'karma'). It is again said therein; "From fixation of the mind in 'dāna' etc. to fixation of the mind in 'prajñā' is evil karma ('māra karma')." Now in this assertion there is no forbidding of practising 'dāna' etc. but what has been forbidden is the addiction of the mind to the ego and I-ism, in the concept of the 'grāhya' (the object to be achieved) and 'grāhaka' (the person who receives or achieves) — that is, the received and the receiver, contrary fixation in the donor's[57] charity ('dāna'). 'Dāna' etc. dependent on contrary fixation is impure, 'māra karma'. Otherwise, 'dhyāna' etc. will also not be worth practising, how will, then, release come about?

Whatever 'dāna' etc. is given because of or by keeping in view the variety of 'sattvas' by the donor ('aupalam-bhika') is impure. Arya Gaganaganja propounds it thus: "'dāna' etc. which indicate differentiation among beings ('sattvas') are the acts of the devil ('māra karma')". So it has been stated in Tri-skandha-pariṇāmanā. "'Dāna'(giving), 'śila' (conduct), 'kśānti' (forbearance) 'veerya' (valour or effort), 'dhyāna' (meditation), 'prajñā' (wisdom), not aware of the 'samatā' (equivalence) of all these by one who falls into obtainment (of 'dāna' etc.), for such a one I teach as to how to protect 'śila' (character) from diseased[58] 'śila' or misconduct (born of) lapses[59] in 'dāna' and 'kśānti-bhāvanā' (contemplation of forbearance) from the nomenclature of 'I' (sva) and 'other' ('para') etc." Here too such giving (dāna) etc. which rises above the contrarities of differentiation ('nānatva'), becomes purified for the giver ('aupalam-bhika'); so has it been propounded and not the forbidding of 'dāna' etc. in toto; otherwise, 'dāna' etc. would have been wholly commended as such, and its descending into contrary obtainment would not have found mention: It has been said in Brahma-pariprichhā also: "all conduct ('charyā') is 'parikalpita'[60] (based on factor or causes) ; 'bodhi alone is without 'hetu' or 'pratyaya' (niṣparikalpa).[61]" Owing to the varying nature of practices for the generation of 'bodhi' (enlightenment), even 'bodhi' is (sometimes) mentioned as 'parikalpita' (created or fashioned). What has been propounded here is that to stay in a state of effortless abstraction is the explanation[62] of the bodhisattva alone and none else's. What has been said is about the uncreatedness of 'dāna' etc. in the ultimate sense and not that no practice (of it) should be performed.

The Buddhas who were honoured by the Lord in Dipankara[63] – avadāna and whose names could not be enumerated in an aeon ('kalpa') (by the lord) were never forbidden from any practice ('charyā') during their bodhisattva period. Dipankara also did not refute any of the lord's 'charyās' However, when he (i.e bodhisattva Dipankara) was noticed, in the state of 'śānta animitta-vihāra' (a state of absolute equipoise and tranquillity) during the eighth 'bhumi', he expounded this (teaching) but there also he did not forbid its practice. The bodhisattva's supreme revelling in the 'animitta'[64] during the eighth 'bhumi' has been forbidden by the Buddhas in Daśabhumiśvara 'lest they may attain their 'nirvāna' here itself'. If no 'charyā' (practice) is to be performed at all, it would negate all that has been said earlier (about the bodhisattva's charyā).

Again, Brahma-paripriсhhā says: "He gives in charity but does not desire its fruit; he guards his 'śila' but it is never superimposed." "O Brahma! become non-returning ('avaivartika')[65] in Buddha dharmas when equipped with four 'dharmas'." What four? Accepting the unlimited 'samsāra', veneration and worship of limitless Buddhas etc. will stand against anything. It is proper to say that practice should be done neither with mild senses ('mridu indriya')[66] nor with sharp senses ('tikśaṇa indriya')[67] alone, for in this way, for the bodhisattvas established in the first stage to the tenth, the 'charyā' (practice) of 'dāna' etc. is generated nor does he roam[68] not in the residual appendices;[69] thus has it been said. It is improper to say that one who has entered the 'bhumi' is of 'soft senses'. As has been stated in Ārya Upāli-paripriсhhā; "Only he who is established in the non-generating 'dharma-kśānti' should practise renunciation ('tyāga'),[70] great renunciation (mahātyāga)[71] and total renunciation ('ati-tyāga').[72]" Sūtra samuchaya also says: 'the bodhisattva, equipped with the attainment of the six perfections, functions through the 'riddhi' (special power) of Tathāgata. There is nothing speedier than the speed of Tathāgata's power. And, for the boddhisattvas, there is no path speedier than that of the six perfections, and the ten 'bhumis'." The sūtra says that mental generation (i.e. tendencies) is refined gradually like the refining of gold. Ārya Lankāvatāra and Daśa-bhumiśvara also state: "When the bodhisattva gets established in 'tathatā' he enters the first 'bhumi'. After that, step by step, he enters the 'Tathāgata bhumi, after refining the preceding 'bhumis'. Therefore, there is no other gateway than that of 'bhumis' and 'pāramitās' (perfections) to simultaneously enter the city of Buddha."

It is improper to say that as all the Six Perfections come within the ambit of 'dhyāna' and that all of them are fulfilled by its practice, so other perfections like dāna etc. need not be practised. If it were so then, owing to the six perfections coming within the ambit of Lord Buddha's (gomaya-maṇḍala)[73] only maṇḍala,[74] should be practised and not 'dhyāna' etc. Even a 'śrāvaka' who has entered the absorption ('samāpatti') of 'nirodha'-sāmādhi[75] will be deemed to have attained the fulfilment of the six perfections through the non-recurrence ('a-samudāchara') of the objective ('nimitta') etc. In that case there will be nothing to proclaim the contrast between the 'śrāvaka' and the bodhisattva. The bodhisattvas must practise the six perfections under all circumstances. In order to substantiate it, the lord has shown the presence of all other 'pāramitās' (perfection) in every single 'pāramitā'. It is said in Sarvadharma-vaipulya; "O Maitreya! about this acquisition of the six perfections which has been spoken of for the enlightenment of bodhisattvas, the ignorant persons would say that the bodhisattvas should be well instructed in the perfection of wisdom ('prajñā-pāramitā') alone, of what avail is his interest in other 'pāramitās'? They regard the other 'pāramitās as 'stained'. Then, O Ajita! do you take that

Kaśirāja (the king of Kaśi) to be a fool (lit. of tainted wisdom) who gave away pieces of his flesh to the falcon in lieu of that of the pigeon? 'No Lord' replied Maitreya. The Lord continued, 'O Maitreya! Whatever 'kuśal-mulas' (root-merits) equipped with six perfections were earned by me while practising the conduct of the bodhisattvas, did they do any harm to me? 'No lord!' replied Maitreya. The lord said, 'O Ajita!' you also practised perfect 'dāna' pāramitā (the perfection of giving) for sixty aeons ('kalpas') and equally practised 'prajñā-pāramitā' (the perfection of Wisdom) for sixty 'kalpas'. Even then, these ignorant persons will say that a single path like that of 'śunyatā alone will lead to enlightenment (bodhi). Such a person will become impure of conduct ('charyā') or practice." While practising 'śunyatā' alone they will enter into the 'śrāvaka's' 'nirvāṇa'. Therefore, 'prajñā must be practised with 'upāyaya'.

Acharya Nāgārjunapāda says in Sūtra-sammuchaya; " A bodhisattva should not practise serious dharmas without the skill of means ('upāyaya')." Herein, the āchārya has expounded what he got from sources like Ārya Vimalakirti-nirdeśa etc. and not that these are the words of Āchārya Nāgārjunapāda (himself). It is not proper for learned observors to forsake the Lord's words which comprise scriptures ('āgama') and logic ('yukti') and accept the words of ignorant fools. It is said in Ārya Ratna-kuta: "Sūnyatā which comprises the blessing of omnipotence and is accompanied by such 'kuśalas' (merits) as giving ('dāna') etc. should be meditated upon as such." And again; "O Kaśyapa! just as the king performs all his functions with the assistance of his minister, so also does the 'prajñā' of the bodhisattvas equipped with the skill of 'upāyaya' perform all the tasks of lord Buddha."

He who practises 'śunyatā' only will not have entry into 'nirvāṇa'. The lord has said in Ārya Tathāgata-guhya sūtra; "One should not practise 'ekānta-nirlāmbana-chitta', i.e. the solitary propless mind; skill in means ('upāyaya') should also be practised." To illustrate this, it is added, "O Kulaputra! just as fire burns only with its requisite material ('upādana') and is quietened in its absence, so also the mind is fired by its prop ('ālambana') and becomes quietened in its absence. The bodhisattva, with his 'prajñā-pāramitā' (perfection of wisdom) honed and equipped with the skill of 'upāyaya' knows how to calm down 'ālambana' but will not calm down the one with benificent roots. In him no 'kleśālambana' (the prop of mental defilements) arises but he is established in the 'prop of perfection' ('paramitā-ālambana') instead. He examines the 'ālambana' of 'śunyatā' but will look to 'mahākaruṇā' (great compassion) as the 'ālambana' for all sattvas. In this way, 'O Kulaputra! the bodhisattva attains the mastery of 'ālambana' with his refined perfection of 'prajñā'(wisdom) and the skill of 'upāyaya' (means)." So saying in detail, he further amplifies; "The bodhisattva has no such 'ālambana' as is not meant for the accumulation of the knowledge of the reality of things, that is, Buddhas 'jñāna' The bodhisattva, all whose 'alāmbanas' get transformed into supreme enlightenment, alone is skilful in 'upāyaya' and such a one sees all 'dharmas' as embracing 'bodhi'. Even then, O Kulaputra! there is nothing in the three thousand or many thousands of 'loka-dhātus' (wordly components) which is not meant for the 'sattvas' enjoyment. O Kulaputra! there is no such 'ālambana' which the skilful-in-effort bodhisattva does not consider useful for his enlightenment." Thus said at length. In this manner, the acquisition of wisdom ('prajñā') and means ('upāyaya') by bodhisattvas has been indicated in an unlimited number of sutras. If he himself cannot start the valorous effort of accumulating 'punya' collection through 'dāna' etc. it is not proper for him to preach it to others as that would be tantamount to deceiving both himself and others.

It has been propounded in the 'yukti' (literature of logic) and 'āgama' (scripture) that the bodhisattvas, after 'bhuta-examination' should make a collection of such 'punya' accumulations as 'dāna' etc. So the wise ones have said that one should forsake like poison the words of egotistical, half-read persons and act in accordance with the nectar like words of such learned scholars as Āacharya Nāgārjuna and others by generating mahākaruṇā for all 'mahāsattvas' remaining unattached as a magician and should endeavour to uplift the whole world through the transformation of all beneficient practices like 'dāna' etc. into 'anuttra-samyaka-sambodhi' (transcendental, supreme enlightenment). It has been said in Ārya Dharma-samgiti, "Just as a magician endeavours to undo his own creation and being already aware of its illusionary aspect, is unattached to it, so also the bodhisattva, conscious of illusionary nature of the three states of existence ('tribhāva') past, present and future and having attained perfect enlightenment is ready (to do his duty) towards the world because he already knows its reality."

In this way, he who constantly practises 'prajñā' and 'upāyaya' with reverence, his mental emanations having gradually matured, more and more of extremely pure 'kśaṇa'[76] is generated for him. His meditation on the meaning of things having attained excellence, he becomes aware of the extremely clear 'dharma dhātu'[77] (the true essence of things) devoid of all fictionality ('kalpanā-jāla'). He attains transcendental knowledge as clear as the calm, windless lamp. He then achieves the 'ālambana' of the ultimate of things and enters the 'daraśana mārga'. He attains the first 'bhumi' (stage). After refining the succeeding stages one after another and removing all accumulated 'āvarṇas' like (refining) gold, attains unattached and unassailable 'jnāna' and reaches 'Buddha bhumi' (the stage of Buddhahood), the foundation of all virtue; also he obtains 'ālambana' in the shape of the fulfilment of his work. Therefore, those who desire 'Buddha-hood' should endeavour to tread the Middle Path.

May all people attain the Middle path as the result of whatever 'punya' (merit) I may have earned by indicating the 'madhya mārga' (middle path) in this way.

Good people, after removing the dirt of jealousy etc. remain insatiate, like the ocean with its waters and, after good examination, continue accepting good words just as the (royal) swan gladly weans milk from water.

Hence, the learned people, after overcoming the prejudices of their minds, should accept good words from even the ignorant.

Here ends the final Bhāvanākrama composed by Āchārya Kamalaśila.

GLOSSARY - I

1. Bhāvanākrama — 'bhāvanā' is meditation; it consists of visualisation and contemplation of a resolve, an object or an idea and strictly meditating on it in accordance with vows undertaken; the sequence of meditational process. For example, 'maitri', 'karuṇā', 'muditā' and 'upekśā' are the four exalted states of the mind. Also called 'brahma-vihāra' the 'bhāvanā' of these four leads the practitioner to 'samyaka' pratipatti or true realisation, his mental defilements having evaporated.
2. 'ādikarmika' — a novice initiate who wishes to pursue the bodhisattva path, of the four-fold tantra quadrangle in Mahāyana-kriyā-tantra, charyā-tantra, yog-tantra and anuttar-tantra — kriyātantra's standard text is Adikarma-pradeep which deals with the rules of initiation and subsequent conduct as prescribed for an 'ādikarmik bodhisattva'
3. sarvajñatā — the knowledge of the true nature of all phenomena, that is, 'nissvabhāvatā'.
4. karuṇā — compassion.
5. bodhichitta — enlightened mind.
6. pratipatti — perception, comprehension.
7. dharmah — disciplines, instructions, practices.
8. bhadanta — an honorific for a realised monk.
9. pūrvangamā — that which goes ahead of a thing; precursor, fore-runner.
10. as at 9 above.
11. adhiṣṭhāna — object of contemplation, focal idea to reflect on.
12. sambhāra — accumulation, collection.
13. trividha dukha — three-fold suffering of body, mind and speech.
14. traidhātuka — beings living in the three worlds of humans, gods and hell dwellers, the earth, the heavens, the hells.
15. pretas — disembodied spirits, 'preta-loka' is one of the six realms of existence after death.
16. tiryaka — another realm of existence where one is born as a dragging, crawling beast.
17. samādhāna-chetsa — of composed mind.
18. praṣma — tranquillity.
19. anusāya — impurity generated by feelings of attachment, lust etc.
20. kāmāvachāra — one who always wanders in the realm of desire or kāma; it is also equated with, 'deva-loka' by some as the gods always dwell in 'kāma'.
21. defilements born of actions.
22. suffering born of samskāras.

23. chitta-samatā — a mental attitude of total equality for all beings; it is achieved through the practice of 'parātma-samatā' or by exchanging your own self with others.
24. sama-pravritta — equitably disposed towards all; equal concern.
25. niṣpanna — complete, full, equanimous.
26. bodhichitta — a mind that aspires after bodhi or the enlightenment of a bodhisattva.
27. prārthnākāram — importunate, solicitous.
28. samyaka-sambodhi — the ultimate or correct knowledge of reality; true cognition of 'bhuta-tathatā'.
29. par-samādāpana — acquiring by others.
30. pratipatti — attainment of supreme knowledge.
31. vajra-ratna — adamantine gem; supreme, impenetrable substance.
32. chittotapada — generating the mind, inducing it towards 'sarvajñatā'.
33. *guṇas* — qualities.
34. śrāvaka — *lit.* hearer.
35. pratyeka-buddha — *lit.* solitary realiser.
36. pāramitā — perfection
37. upāyaya — means, practice.
38. dāna-pāramitā — perfection of giving.
39. parjña-pāramitā — perfection of wisdom.
40. praṇidhi — vow, fixing the mind with determination.
41. kuśala-mula — practices that lead to meritorious action, root-merit.
42. anumodana — commending.
43. sādharaṇani — common, ordinary.
44. Buddha-dharma — pratices enjoined on a bodhisattva.
45. bodhi-sambhāra — accumulation of the attributes of enlightenment.
46. vipāka — fruit, result in maturation of actions done.
47. ākāśa-dhātu — the element of space or sky.
48. buddha-kśetraṇi — Buddha-fields, believed to be two dozen in number; the Mahāyāna concept of the presence of more than one Buddha simultaneously presiding in their own 'lokas' or worlds, their 'kśetras' (fields) like the sukha-vati-vyuha of Amitabha Buddha.
49. pranidhi-chitta — a mind fixed on the goal of achieving bodhi.
50. Prasthān-chitta — a mind ready to travel on the path of bodhi.
51. samvar — vow.
52. sambhāra — collection, accumulation.
53. kalyāṇa-mitra — jinas, bodhisattvas, realised ones, A kalyāṇa-mitra is described as one who is capable of instructing in serious themes and is equipped with extraordinary attributes, the foremost of

'kalyāṇa-mitras' is Lord Buddha himself as revealed by him to Ānanda in the following words: *'mama hi Ānanda kalyāṇmitramaagmya 'jāti-dharmāh sattvah 'jati-dharmama parimunchanti'.*

54. Manjuśri as Ambara-rāja; the story of.
55. apramāṇa — the four cordial virtues of 'maitri', 'karuṇā', 'muditā' and 'upekśā' — the 'brahma-vihāras' — have been designated by the scriptures as 'apramāṇa', because they are limitless and everlasting and they wash away the dirt of attachment, envy jealousy and ill-will so that the bodhisattva may practise 'parahita' or others' well-being.
56. samgraha-vastu — comprises the four-fold acquisition of love, compassion, joy and detachement, the 'brahma-vihāras'.
57. 'śilpa' — craft.
58. upāyaya — *lit.* approaching, coming near, means; it also refers to compassion or 'bhuta-dayā' and to that state of samādhi in which 'prajñā' is born. In the latter state it is 'upāyaya pratyaya'.
59. samgrah-vastu — see 56 above.
60. kśetra-pariśudhi — purification of the (bodhisattva's) field.
61. bahu-parivśra sampata — the wealth of a large family or entourage of disciples.
62. sattva paripāka-nirmāṇa — helping maturation of sattvas meritorious acts.
63. samkleśa — defilements.
64. samgrah-jñāna — the knowledge of cultivating 'maitri', karuṇā, 'mudita and upekśā'.
65. parichheda — analysis, discrimination.
66. bhumi — stage, level.
67. daśa-bhumi — ten stages of a bodhisattva's 'sādhana', 'muditā', 'vimalā', 'prabhākari', 'archiṣmati', 'sudurjayā', 'abhimukti', 'durangmā', 'achalā', 'sādhumati' and 'dharma-megha'.
68. aṣtama-bhumi — 'achala' or steadfast, the eighth stage of boddhisattva-hood.
69. vyuthāna — the fourth of the five steps for the resolve to rise up from a balanced 'dhyāna' after a desired span of time, because the first dhyāna is not without its inherent shortcomings; the resolve to rise above these is 'vyuthāna'.
70. achalā — the eighth 'bhumi' in which the seeker fully understands the nissvabhāvatā of things and is not affected by the pleasures of the body, the mind and the speech, he remains 'achala', immovable, steadfast.
71. dharma-mukha-srota — the source of all dharma practice.
72. upasamhāra — conclusion, finish.

73. kśānti — one of the six perfections; in this context it is 'faith' - 'śradhā' with 'ruchi' or interest in the pursuit of vows.
74. daśa-bala — an epithet of lord Buddha who possessed ten singularly distinct powers; knowledge of all places, knowledge of all time, knowledge of all the different spheres, knowledge of all different kinds of emancipation, knowledge of other's conduct, knowledge of the good and evil force of karma, knowledge of the obstacles from kleśas and the absorption of dhyāna, knowledge of previous lives; has pure, divine eyes and is capable of destroying all defilements.
75. chatur-vaiśārda — four great attributes ascribed to Lord Buddha; 1. his body was 'anāsrva', pure, made up of flawless substances and attributes; 2. he could assume unlimited 'rūpakāyas' and bodies simultaneously at different places, 3. his powers were immeasurable. 4. his glory and effulgence had no bounds.
76. śānti-vimokśa-vihāra — the state of calm abiding.
77. jñāna-mukhāchintytā — a state of peace and steadiness born of 'jñāna'.
78. dharmatā — the nature of dharmas or all phenomena which is 'nissvabhāvatā' or 'śunyatā'.
79. tathāgata — one who has realised the 'tathatā' or 'as it-ness' of things, the 'as-it-ness' being their insubstantial non-true existence; hence 'tathatā' is identical with 'paramārtha satya'.
80. dharma-dhātu — the essence of all 'dharmatā' which is 'śunyatā'; it is indentical with 'bhuta-koti', 'tathatā' etc. 'dhātu' comprises factors which join up to produce a phenomena and there are eighteen 'dhātus' - six senses, six object, six cognitions. Of the six object - dhātus the last is 'dharma-dhātu', which in itself comprises sixty four dharmas.
81. sarvadharma śunyatā — the emptiness of all phenomena.
82. sarva-dharmānuplabdhi — the non-existence of all phenomena.
83. avikalpa-dharmatā — to understand the true nature of phenomena; 'vikalpa' is defined as 'āsrava partantra' or unclean dependent as it is born of 'partyayas'; to rise above it is 'anāsrava vikalpa' or the unblemished alternative or 'avikalpa', the opposite of 'vikalpa'.
84. apramāṇatā — There are ten dharmas of a handsome mind (śobhana chaitska); 'śradhā' 'apramāda', 'prasrabdhi', 'apekśā', 'hri' 'apatrapa' 'alobha' 'advesa' 'maitri' and 'ahimsā'. 'Apramāṇa' is one of the four divisions of 'śobhana chaitsika' and comprises 'karuṇā' and 'muditā'; 'apramāṇata' is handsome, inimitable quality or nature.
85. abhinirhāra -- accumulation, appropriation; the various 'bhumis'

are also called 'vihāras' because the bodhisattvas roam about in them for the 'abhinirhāra' of 'kuśala' or merit.

86. prabhā-maṇḍala — halo, aura of light around a divine being.
87. svarānga-viśudhi — refinement of speech, in mantra recitation.
88. nirvikalpa — undifferentiated, transcendental without an alternative or 'vikalpa'.
89. paryanta-gāmi — unlimited, extending in all directions, infinite.
90. aparyanta — limitless.
91. aparyanta — eternal
92. apramāṇa-kśetra — the fields of illimitable compassion of a bodhisaṭtva.
93. apramāṇa-sattva — unlimited hordes of sentient beings.
94. apramāṇa dharma-vibhaktata — illimitable variety and division of dharmas and their analyses.
95. abhinirhāra dwāra — door or entrance to the accumulation of merit.
96. abhinirhāra karma — action that leads to accumulation of karma.
97. adhimukti — final release from cyclic existence; also means 'faith' or 'śraddhā'.
98. avabodha — true enlightenment or knowledge of the ultimate truth of all phenomena.
99. sarvajña-jñānabhinirhāra — the garnering of the knowledge of 'sarvajñatā' or of the ultimate truth of things, their 'nissvabhāvatā'.
100. parinirvāṇa — release from cyclic existence.
101. pratisrabdhi — retardation.
102. āvaraṅ — upper crust, cover or lid of 'avidyā' (ignorance) or 'pratitya' (the apparent) which hinders cognition of the reality or 'yathābhuta jñāna' of phenomena.
103. pratikśepa karma — contrary, contradictory action; neglecting etc.
104. śobhana samjñā — fair, correct cognition.
105. aśobhana ṣamjnā — incorrect, ugly, unbecoming cognition.
106. pratikśapti — retards, obstructs.
107. samudāgama — cultivation, generation.
108. upāyaya-pāramitā — perfection of 'karuṇā' or compassion.
109. Ajit — name of a bodhisattva.
110. Kaśirāja — King 'Śivi' of Varāṇasi whose compassion was put to test by god Indra; the latter in the guise a of preying falcon, pounced on a pigeon; he offered to cut a piece of his own flesh as compensation to the falcon if it released its prey from its talons; when put in the scales the pigeon grew heavier and heavier in weight and the compassionate king went on slicing pieces of his flesh; finally, the god resumed his original form, blessed and congratulated Kāśirāja and made him whole before disappearing.

111. Maitreya — a bodhisattva.
112. Kalpa — cosmic period; a fabulous period of time comprising thousands of years of mortals' time calculation; at the end of a 'kalpa', the world is annihilated.
113. naya — system or path; Mahāyāna consists of two 'nayas'; 'pāramitā-naya' and 'mantra-naya'. It is said that Lord Buddha taught the former at gridhra-kuta and the latter at 'śri-parvata'.
114. Paryavāsna — end, conclusion.
115. pratisthāpita — installed, established.
116. rūpa-kāyā — material form; also called 'nirmāṇa-kāyā', the historical form of 'sākyamuni' which he assumed for the world.
117. kśetra — field, domain.
118. parivāra — progeny, continuum, entourage.
119. viparyāsa — contrariety, delusion which makes one believe as real or true what is unreal or untrue.
120. anta — limit.
121. samāropa — superimposition.
122. apavāda — refutation, negation, contradiction.
123. lakśaṇa — attributes, marks, signs; the 32 ordinary and 80 special marks of Lord Buddha.
124. anuvyanjanā — expression.
125. abhisamaya — true 'jñāna'; it has two stages; 'dharma-kśānti' i.e. passion for dharma and 'dharma-darśana' or experiencing dharma.
126. dharma-kāyā — the subtle form of Lord Buddha which is incorporeal, indescribable 'paramārthic' in essence and is the equivalent to 'śunyatā'.
127. sambhava — generation, creation.
128. udagrahaṇa — grasping, taking up, holding onto.
129. unmārga — deviation, wrong road.
130. vyapadeśa — appellation, designation.
131. samādhi — a state of meditational absorption; 'samyaka ādheiyte ekāgri-kriyate' 'vikśepana'.
132. śrutamayi — listening to and reading of scriptures etc.
133. āgama — collection of scriptures.
134. chintāmayi — reflective, contemplative.
135. neetārtha — intelligible meaning.
136. neyartha — dubious meaning.
137. bhutārtha — that which has actually happened, real facts.
138. abhutārtha — not a fact.
139. vichikitsā — doubt, uncertainty.
140. tirthika — those belonging to non-buddhistic schools of thought like 'samkhya', 'vaiseṣika', 'nirgrantha' and 'ājivakas'.

141. nairātamya — the theory of non-soul; there is no permanent entity as 'ātma'.
142. anutpād — non-generation, non-creation.
143. utpāda — generation, creation.
144. abhiniveśa — adherence to, relying on.
145. yoniśa — abstract meditation by which one realises 'anitya' and 'anātmā'.
146. yoni — path.
147. yoniśa prichhā — inquiring into the paramārthic state of phenomena.
148. chakāra-mukha — empty.
149. abhāva-mukha — non-existent by nature.
150. Īśvara — the vedic concept of a supreme, omnipotent god.
151. kramśa — one after the other.
152. nirapekśattvāta — owing to independence.
153. artha-kriyā — action performed with a special purpose; it aims at the attainment of the 'artha' (objective) and the giving up of the 'anartha' (non-essential).
154. samāropa — superimposition.
155. asata — that which is not.
156. ākāśa — space, void, Nagarjuna believed it to be beyond both 'bhāva' and 'abhāva'
157. nirodh — lit. 'cessation', the third of the four 'ārya-satyaṣ', it too is beyond bhāva and 'abhāva'.
158. avyavadhāna — no-interval or interim.
159. kśaṇa — lit. 'moment'.
160. pinda — mass, body.
161. sāvayava — lit. 'with limbs', alive active.
162. samvriti satya — apparent but illusory truth as distinguished from 'paramārtha satya' or the ultimate truth of things.
163. vijnanā-cognition, skandha — lit. (heap), bundle, aggregate, 'vijñāna' skandha' is one of the five such aggregates, the other four being those of 'rūpa', 'vedanā', 'samjñā' and 'samskāra'.
164. aleeka — falsehood, meaningless.
165. māyā — delusion.
166. nirabhilāṣa — without bias.
167. pratipatti — acquisition, comprehension, meditative realisation.
168. prithvi-kritsna — the first of the ten 'kritsnas'; the sanskrit 'kritsna' becomes 'kasana' in pali, thus 'prithvi kritsna' generally came to be called 'prithvi kasana' or 'kasina'; Pali 'patthvi kaṣana'; there are forty 'karmasthānas', ten krisṇas, ten aśubhas, ten 'anusmritis' four 'brahma-vihāras', four 'ārupya', one 'samjñā' and one 'vyuthāna'. Why are 'kritsnas' so called? Because they attract the

meditative aspects of the 'kritsna' (or entire) mind (chitta). In 'prithvi kritsna', the first of the eight dhyānas, the object of concentration is an earthen pot at a lonenly place, extending the sādhaka's reflective process to all names and synonyms of earth ('prithvi'); the exercise of dhyāna through 'kritsna' is called 'karma-kasina'.

169. 'śamatha' — a state of total tranquillity; calm abiding.
170. samāhita — one of a sedate mind; meditative equipoise; balanced.
171. adhivāsana — commending, awareness.
172. veerya — persevering effort.
173. śila — conduct, to be cultivated as one of the six perfections.
174. pāpa-deśana — indicating, confessing, stating, one's sins or faults, it is the first step in bodhicharyā.
175. punyānumodana — commending the qualities of virtuous living.
176. padmāsana — sitting crosslegged in lotus posture; one of the more comfortable 'āsanas' or postures for meditation.
177. vikśepa doṣa — distraction; ignorance which leads to illusionary views; one of the 'kleśa-mahābhaumikas'.
178. ālambaṇa — an apparent, palable mental prop or support for sādhanā; for example, a 'ghata' (piture) as an accessory aid for dhyāna.
179. śunyata is of 18 types (though according to Haribhadra, it is of 20 types) as follows; adhyātma śunyatā, bahirdhā, śunyatā-śunyatā, mahā, paramārtha, samskrita, asamskrita, atyanta, anavarāgra, prakriti, sarvadharma, lakśaṇa, upalambha, abhāva-svabhava, bhāva, abhāva, svabhāva and parabhāva 'śunyatā'.
180. vastubheda — is of two kinds; 'śuddha' and 'parikalpita'. The first is paramārtha state and the second a deviation from it being based on 'kalpanā' or imagination.
181. abhidharma — the third 'pitaka' or basket of Lord Buddha's word, so called because of its three attributes of 'abhikśṇyāta (ability to elucidate many facets of the some dharma), 'abhibhavāta' (ability to refute other beliefs), and 'abhigatitā' (ability to offer a tangible exposition of the tenets of Buddha-dharma).
182. styāna — lassitude.
183. akarmaṇyatā — do-nothing-ness; cowardice.
184. samvega — detachment.
185. abhisamskāra — refining, variation.
186. sva-rasa-vāhi — of its own volition.
187. ābhoga — effort.
188. satyābhoga — true effort.
189. sama-pravritti — 'sama' is second of the five steps by which complete control over first dhyāna is achieved; tendency towards

'sama' or balance.

190. vikśepa — one of the ten 'kleśa-mahabhaumikas'; described as 'klista-samādhi' or complicated, confused samādhi.
191. samanvāharana — withdrawal of the senses from the world.
192. doṣa — fault, shortcoming.
193. kausidya — sloth, it is the opposite of 'veerya'.
194. ālambana sampramoṣa — forsaking the (meditational) prop or support.
195. laya — mental lethargy, inert absorption.
196. audhatya — insolence, arrogance.
197. anābhoga — effortless.
198. ābhoga — effort.
199. prahāna samskāra — tendency to eradicate.
200. śraddhā — faith; it is called 'chitta-prasāda'.
201. chhanda — the desire to act, perform, it has been defined as 'kartu-kāmyatā'.
202. vyayāma — hard work, industriousness.
203. prasrabdhi — activeness of body and mind in yoga-sādhanā.
204. smriti — non-forgetfulness.
205. samprajñāya — awareness, mental alertness.
206. chetanā — it is defined as that consciousness which refines the mind.
207. upekśā — detachment.
208. abhisamaya pratyaya — factors that lead to 'samyaka' or true jñāna; comprises two parts; 'dharma-kśānti' or generation of interest (ruchi) in dharma and 'dharma-jñāna' or the actual knowledge of (or personally experienced) dharma.
209. anābhoga — without effort.
210. ābhoga — effort, it is also defined as 'anyayāna mansikāra' or contemplation of other paths.
211. riddhi — prosperity, affluence.
212. karmaṇyatā — skill, the ability to perform.
213. arupi-samāpatti — absorption in the formless aspect in dharma meditation, 'samāpatti loka' consists of 'rūpa-loka' and 'arūpa-loka', the sattvas possessing healthy, beautiful bodies in the former and being without form in the latter; their realisation is in accordance with the state of 'samāpatti'.
214. vimokśa — deliverance, release.
215. vedanā — feeling; the second of the five 'skandhas'.
216. anāgamya — inaccessible, undefined.
217. prathama dhyāna — 'samādhi' is of two types; 'upachāra' and 'arpaṇā'; of forty 'karma-sthānas' ten help in achieving 'upachāra' or what may be called 'peripheral samādhi'; the

remaining thirty 'karmasthānas' help in attaining 'arpaṇā' or 'absolute samādhi.

The first dhyāna is achieved through five steps; 1. āvarjana — fixing the mind in meditation for a specified period. 2. 'sama' — to fix dhyāna in the five aspects of 'vitarka', 'vichāra' 'priti', 'sukha' and 'ekāgratā'. 3. 'adhiṣthāna' — the ability to fix dhyāna in a trice (ten times 'sphota' or clicking of fingers). 4. 'vyuthāna' — ability to rise up from dhyāna after a specified period; 5. 'pratyaveksana' ability to analyse and observe clearly what occurs from dhyāna.

218. abhibhava — dominant, powerful.
219. āyatana — door, entrance.
220. ākara — form.
221. ātma-samjñā — body consciousness.
222. udreka — excessive, overwhelming.
223. chitta-mātra — *lit.* 'mind only'; term used as a synonym of yogāchāra school.
224. tathatā — *lit.* 'such-ness', things as they are in the ultimate analysis; term used as the equivalent to paramārtha tattva, 'supreme enlightenment, 'śunyatā' etc.
225. nirābhāsa — *lit.* 'without splendour', formless; without fallacious appearance.
226. nairātmya-jñāna — the knowledge of the non- self doctrine of dharmas, of the ultimately non-substantial nature of things.
227. avyatireka — dissimilarity; difference.
228. advya jñāna — the knowledge of the non-duality of things; ultimate 'jñāna'.
229. paramatattva — ultimate essence; supreme truth of all phenomena.
230. samayaka jñāna — correct or right knowledge.
231. vaikalya — bafflement; confusion.
232. asamjñi samāpatti — meditational equipoise or samādhi attainable by the yogi in the fourth Dhyāna, or release; in fact, the result of this 'samāpatti' is not 'utpatti' but 'nirodha' like a 'setu' or bridge over a river serving to retard the flow.
233. rāga — vehement desire; attachment.
234. timira-doṣa — clouded eyesight; kind of blindness; catract; one who suffers from it is called 'taimarika'.
235. yuganadha — united, two-fold.
236. upalambha — acquirement.
237. anupalambha — non-acquirement.
238. avasthāna lakśṇa — staidness.
239. anābhoga — satiety.
240. prapancha — deceit; fraud.

241. bhava — comprises two things; 'vyavahāra-ākara' and 'dharma-trāta guna, i.e. change due to change of 'avastha' or situation in a dharma and the basic quality or characteristic of a dharma.
242. a-bhāva — also of two kinds; 'buddhi pūrvaka' and 'abuddhi - pūrvaka' i.e. the is-not-ness of a thing due it, extinction and the act of constant extinction.
243. tri-kāla — past, present and future.
244. vyāpattva — permeableness.
245. vyāpaka — pervading.
246. vyāpya — permeable.
247. jñeyāvaraṇa — cover of ignorance which impedes the dawn of jñāna.
248. kleśāvaraṇa — cover of mental defilements.
249. samvriti — two types of truth — the one that is apparent but is not the truth and the one that is not apparent but is the ultimate truth — 'samvriti satya' and 'paramārtha satya'; the first is aid to discover the latter.
250. samkalpa, vikalpa — will, counter-will, premise, counter-premise.
251. ayoniśa mansikāra — an unmeditational mentalisation wherein 'anitya' is not viewed as 'anitya' etc.
252. driṣti-paryuthhāna — distraction of eyes or sight from dhyāna.
253. viparyāsa — reversion; overthrow.
254. vijñāna — cognitive insight.
255. achintya — *lit.* 'beyond thinking', subtle, un-definable.
256. abhisamaya-gotra buddhi — 'gotra' is caste or class; the gotra is decided in accordance with the 'śubha' and 'aśubha' seeds or the quantity of 'gunas' of a practitioner; of the five 'gotras' enumerated in Mahavyutpatti 'śrāvakayāna abhisamaya gotra' is the first; 'abhisamya' means 'seeing the satyas in 'anasrava' or pure form.
257. niryāṇa — going out, departure, release.
258. a-niryāṇa — non-release.
259. vyāvartana — averting; turning away from.
260. kudristi — *lit.* bad sight; heterodox, philosophical doctrine.
261. skandha — *lit.* 'heap' five aggregates of the world of names or forms; the five 'skandhas' are 'rūpa', 'vedanā', 'samjñā', 'samskāra' and 'vijnāna'.
262. pudgala nairātmya — non-self nature of beings.
263. trai-dhātuka — the concept of the division of the world into the three aggregates of 'kāma-dhātu', 'rūpa-dhātu' and 'arūpa-dhātu' — the world of desire, the world of forms, the world without forms; 'dhātu' means aggregates of the same class.
264. vijñapti — it is 'chitta', 'manasa', 'vijnana'; according to

Vijñānavāda, 'trai-dhātuka is also a 'vikalpa' of the mind ('chitta'); this 'vikalpa' is called 'vijñāna'; all dharmas and the imagined 'self' are the result of 'vijñāna' or 'vijñapti'.

265. vijñāna-vādi — one who believes in the yogāchāra or vijñāna-vāda school; he regards 'vijñāna', i.e. 'chitta' 'manasa' and 'buddhi' as the only 'satya' (true) 'padārtha' (thing), because 'buddhi' alone can observe all things to be in-substantial.
266. anta — end, boundary, limits; the two 'antas' are the 'beginning' and the 'end'.
267. utpada-bhang — generation, creation, — break in.
268. pratitya-samutpāda — dependent origination, chain of causation which brings about an uninterrupted flux of phenomena; it is depicted as a wheel with twelve spokes, the twelve 'nidānas' (links) of creation.
269. jagata — from the root 'gama' (gachha) to go; hence 'jagata' is that which moves, the entire world of beings and things.
270. jñāna-māyā — illusion generated by knowledge.
271. nirmita, nirmāṇa — created; the first of the four-fold wealth of the fruits of 'dharma-kāya' and it consists of the generation of great 'bāhya sampata' (material prosperity).
272. kautūhalama — curiosity, unusual phenomena, curious frivolity.
273. sambodhi — true enlightenment.
274. tri-bhava — the three states ('bhāvas') in which a pudgala functions — 'ateeta bhava' (past), 'pratyutpanna bhava' (present) and 'anāgata bhava' (future).
275. anabhisamskāra — immaculate state.
276. adhimukti bhumi — the first of the ten stages of a bodhisattva; in this he realises 'pudgal nairātmya' and his 'driṣti' becomes pure.
277. adhimukti — devotion; devotional surrender is the root of a bodhisattva's 'adhimukti'.
278. vedanā — feeling, it arises from touch or contact ('sparśa'); there are five bodily ('kayiki') 'vedanās' born of the five senses, one mental ('chaitski') or 'vedanās' born of the mind.
279. samjñā — that state of consciousness through 'sukha-dukha' joy and suffering — when one sees objects as they are.
280. samskāra — the fourth 'skandha' the volitional aspect of aggregates; *lit.* 'mental constituents' gathered from previous lives through good and bad karma.
281. nirodha — cessation.
282. samudaya — generation, aggregation.
283. bhadracharyā — conduct behoving a noble practitioner.
284. dāna — giving; one of the six perfections.
285. anuttara samyaka-sambodhi — supreme transcendental enlighten-

ment.

286. tri-śikśā' — also called 'visuddhi mārga, comprising 'śila-śikśā', 'samādhi śikśā' and 'prajñā' — teachings on conduct, meditation and wisdom.
287. purva-gāmini — leading.
288. hetu — cause, when one 'dharma' is the direct cause of another 'dharma' (phemenon), it is called 'hetu pratyaya', causal factor.
289. pratyaya — factor; its four types are, 'hetu pratyaya', 'samānantar pratyaya', 'ālambana pratyaya' and 'adhipati pratyaya'.
290. nidāna — links; twelve links of causation.
291. purvangmā — forerunner.
292. āyatana — entrance, door, there are twelve 'āyatanas'.
293. rūpa-kāyā — also called 'nirmāṇa kāyā', the Buddha's physical body with which he serves the cause of the 'sattvas' well-being, preaches 'dhyāna', 'samādhi', 'dāna', 'śila', 'prajñā' etc.; it is endless in number, the historical sakyamuni having been one such emanation.
294. samjnā — awareness of an object.
295. akśaya — perpetual.
296. dwādaśāvastha viśeṣa — twelve special stages of 'pratitya samutpāda' mentioned by the Lord in Dvadaśānga-sūtra.
297. bhūmis — stages of a boddhisattva's 'sādhanā'.
298. Buddha-bhūmi — the final stage of supreme absorption and enlightenment which is both immeasurable and unlimited.
299. driḍhatar adhimukti — firmer faith.
300. māra — the evil one, the tempter, the arch demon who tries to wean away a 'sādhaka' from his path. He was overcome by Lord Buddha during his final moments of enlightenment.
301. dhāraṇi — mystic 'mantras' adopted from the sūtra; prayers addressed to Buddha, bodhisattvas and Tara; has protective potency through ritualistic practice during disease and famine etc.
302. vimokśa — release, emancipation.
303. abhijñā — supernatural faculty of Buddhas and boddhisattvas of six kinds taking any form at will; hearing upto any distance; seeing upto any distance; penetrating others' thoughts, knowing everybody's antecedents; freedom from the fear of cyclic rounds.
304. mridu — one of the three types of 'kśānti' or 'ruchi' (interest) in the discovery of the meaning of 'ārya satyas'; such interest is born from 'murdhana' or 'śirṣa' (the top) of four 'kuśala mulas' (root-merits).
305. madhya — as above (304).
306. adhimātra — as above (304).
307. adhimātratā — the generation of 'laukika agradharmas' which are

transitory and unclean in content and have their support in 'dukha' born of desires ('kāmāpta dukha').

308. nirvedha-bhāgiya — the capacity to properly probe and analyse 'satyas' and destroy all doubts; so called owing to the probing faculty or the power to pirece being unassailable.
309. ūṣmagata — the fire (ūṣma) which burns away the kleśa fuel; considered to be one of the root merits ('kuśala mula').
310. mūrdhana — it is synonymous with 'prakarṣa' or upward rise, generates 'kśānti' (interest), the apex of four 'kuśala mūlas'.
311. vridhāloka samādhi — enhanced-light stage of meditation.
312. kśānti-nirvedhiya — capable of being analysed througḥ 'kśānti'.
313. eka-deśa-praviṣta samādhi — medatational state of one-pointedness.
(Note: the four 'nirvedha-bhāgiya' are the four 'kuśala-mulas', 'ūṣmagata', 'mūrdhana', 'kśānti' ('ruchi') 'agradharmas'; 'agrardharma's are dharmas pertaining to 'Agra-yāna' or Mahāyaña').
314. agradharma nirvedha-bhāgiya — the faculty of probing into and pursuing the boddhisattva's dharmas.
315. anantarya samādhi — innermost absorption in 'anantarya mārga' or 'pramāṇa', the yogi first realises the truth about 'kāmadhātu' and in the very first moment is shorn of doubt.
316. angāni — components, parts; also the synonym of 'hetu' (cause).
317. agradharma — the charya or the conduct of the boddhisattva.
318. darśana-mārg — the path of constant practice which refines one's vision but does not totally uproot attachment and envy; the yogi rises up from the 'darśna mārga' to enter the bhāvanā mārga; darśana mārga initiates the yogi into the search for the meaning of the four noble truths with the resolve: I will know.
319. pramuditā — joyousness.
320. samudāgamatā — arising, generation.
321. dharmadhātu — also called 'dharmāyatana', 'vedanā skandha', 'samjñā', 'samsakāra' and 'avijñapti' and the three 'asamskrita' — these seven constitute 'dharmadhātu'.
322. dvitiya bhumi — second stage of a boddhisattva's sādhanā.
323. angas — components.
324. a-samudāchāra — non-generation.
325. sūtra-dhāraṇā — remembering spiritual teachings and oral instructions by memorising them.
326. jalpa — frivolity of speech.
327. satyas — the noble truths of suffering, the cause of suffering, the cessation of suffering and the way to non-suffering.
328. nimitta — it succeeds 'darśna' practices, it is the seed result in the

'adhyātma' sense of initial cognition.

329. nirvatsaha — lazy, inactive.
330. nischhidra animittavihāra — wandering in the state of un-diluted absorption.
331. dharma-deśanā — instructions in dharma.
332. paryāya — equivalence; factors.
333. nirukti — derivation.
334. samvida — insight, understanding.
335. buddha-kśetra — Buddha field.
336. parishata — 'parivāra', creation, entourage.
337. nirmāṇa — the creation of extraordinary apparent objects; the equivalent of 'māyā' (illusion), 'svapna' (dream), 'marichikā' (mirage), 'bimba' (reflection); example: turning pebble into a gold nugget.
338. sattva-paripāka — maturation of the beings' well-being through meritorious deeds.
339. loka-dhātu — consists of 'kāma-dhātu', 'rūpa-dhātu' and 'arūpa-dhātu'.
340. skandha-pariśuddhi — cleansing of the impurities born of five 'skandhas'.
341. nirmāṇa-vaśita — power of practising total 'nirmāṇa'.
342. asakta — detached.
343. apratihata — invulnerable.
344. svayamabhu Buddha — 'ādi-buddha', this concept finds mention in Kāranda-vyuha sūtra as the creator of the world; 'svayambhu' or 'ādinātha' was there before the world and from his samādhi he produced the 'jagata'; Avalokiteśvara was a 'sattva' of 'svayamabhu Buddha who helped create the world; the sun and the moon were born out of Avalokiteśvara's eyes, Maheśvara from the forehead, Brahma from the shoulder and Nārāyaṇa from the heart.
345. sambhoga-kāyā — subtler than his nirmāṇa-kāyā, this body of Lord Buddha is very effulgent and ever emanates golden rays, through this body the lord gave his Mahayāna-sūtra sermon on Gridhra-kuta (Vulture Peak) and in Sukhāvati.
346. nirmāṇa-kāyā — the purely physical body of Lord Buddha in which he manifests himself for ministering to the well-being of 'sattvas'; it can manifest itself in innumerable forms and the historical Sākyamuni was one such.
347. dharma-kāyā — the 'paramārtha' or subtle body of Lord Buddha, it is enternal ('ananta'), immeasurable ('aparmeya') and indescriable (anirvachaniya); it is the same in the case of all the Buddhas, everlasting ('nitya') true ('satya') and of unlimited

attributes ('ananta guṇa-yukta') it is the lord's true body, the equivalent of 'tathatā', 'dharma-dhātu', 'tathāgata-garbha' etc.

GLOSSARY - II

1. Kumārabhuta — *lit.* 'one ever young'; one of the epithets of Manjuśri, the bodhisattva of wisdom.
2. sarvajñatā — *lit.* 'omniscence'; in Mahāyāna parlance it denotes the 'jñāna' of the ultimate nature of all dharmas which is 'nissvabhāvatā'.
3. hetu — *lit.* 'cause'; certain factors ('pratyaya') combine with the main cause or 'hetu' to produce a certain result ('hetuphala').
4. pratigha — hindrance, obstruction.
5. nirapekśa-bhāva — detachment.
6. abhrānta — unequivocal, not dubious.
7. avikala — steadfast.
8. hetu-pratyayas — causal factors; for example the seed could be called the 'hetu' and the earth, the sun, the water, which help the seed to sprout, are the 'pratyayas'.
9. vineya-jana — those to be instructed; pupils.
10. pariavasāna — end, termination.
11. sambhāra — accumulation, collection.
12. sattva-dhātu — the world of sentient beings.
13. ayogriha — house made of lac.
14. pravritti — inclination, tendency.
15. samśara — the cyclic rounds of birth and death.
16. madhyastha-bhāva — even-mindedness.
17. saralatā — ease, felicity, simplicity.
18. chitta-santāna — tendicies of mind.
19. trividha dukha — triple suffering; 'daihika' (bodily), 'daivika' (destined) and 'bhautika' (worldly).
20. kārpaṇya — poverty, penury.
21. upaghāta — hurt, stroke, violation.
22. kudriṣti — *lit.* 'faulty vision'; a heterodox philosophical vision.
23. prapāta — sheer fall, precipice.
24. viparināma — ripening, transformation.
25. kāmāvachara — the sattva who roams about in 'kama-dhātu' or the realm of desires.
26. madhyapakśa — middle way.
27. the ten directions are; the four cardinal directions, four subsidiary directionṣ and zenith and nadir.
28. niṣpanna — complete.
29. chiṭṭotpāda — generation of mind.
30. anuttar samyaka-sambodhi — transcendental enlightenment.
31. samvara — *lit.* 'detachment' or 'virati', the vows to practise 'śila' and detachment.

32. 'śila-parivartan — a text on the subject of 'śila' transformation.
33. anuśaya — feeling or 'bhāva' it is that which helps 'karma' to ripen, the root of 'bhava' (birth) and 'punarbhava' (rebirth); lit. to grow, to fructify.
34. udraka — known as Udraka-Rama-putra, a well-known ascetic to whom prince Siddartha went after renouncing his home; not satisfied with the answer to his questions by Ānanda Kalāma, the first asectic he had approached, he repeated his queries to the Samkhaya master, Udraka; not satisfied with his answers too, Siddhartha went to the 'aśvathha' tree to meditate.
35. paryāya — synonym; equivalent.
36. Vinay — rule; Lord Buddha's words about rules and regulations of conduct for 'Bhikśus' and others are collected in Vinay-pitaka.
37. dukha-skandha — dukha heaps.
38. anukūla — beneficial, efficacious.
39. cheevara — a buddhist monk's garment or cloak.
40. prakriti — diversion, disturbance.
41. pratikśepa — repudiation, contradiction.
42. śrāvaka samvara — 'śrāvaka' vows.
43. pratividhāna — precaution, prevention; counteracting.
44. pārājika — the four pārājika dharmas are stealing, killing, unchastity and falsely claiming superhuman powers; one guilty of these four.
45. dvadaśānga — twelve points or aspects stressed in Lord Buddha's discourses probably refers to 'Dvādaśānga-sūtra' which deals with the exposition of the twelve 'angas' of 'pratitya-samutpāda'.
46. neetārtha sūtra — intelligible sūtras.
47. neyārtha sūtra — dubious of interpretation sūtras.
48. śringātaka — cross-ways; road junction; a point where several roads meet.
49. bodhi-manda — adorned with bodhi.
50. paryanka — squatting posture; doubling of legs.
51. Bhatāraka Vairochaṇa — name of a Tathāgata; 'bhattāraka' is an honorific for a worship-worthy, venerable scholar; 'vairochana' means the illuminator.
52. sukhāsana — comfortable seat.
53. prīti — peace and contentment of body and mind; it is of five types; 'kṣudrika' which creates horripilation, 'kśaṇika', which is like a lightning flash moment by moment; 'avakrāntikā', which overwhelms like sea waves; 'avakrānta' which disappears like sea waves; 'udvega', which is full of tremendous force; 'sphuraṇa', which is long-lasting and permeates the whole body.
54. geya — *lit.* 'that which can be sung', one of the metres of 'ārya-

jāti' 'chhandas'.

55. vyākaraṇa — one of the nine 'angas' of 'sūtra-pitaka'; herein Lord Buddha foretold about the future degradation of 'bhikśus'.
56. gāthā — lyrical ballads; stories of 'bhikśus' and bhikśunis in prose and verse.
57. undāna — highly elevating words of the Lord, collected into eight parts of Udāna-varga, also contains parables.
58. nidāna — stories.
59. avadāna — *lit.* 'biography', contains the lives of great buddhist monks.
60. iti-virttaka — divided into 112 divisions in mixed prose and verse, contain the teachings of the Lord in earlier times.
61. jātaka — about 550 tales of Buddha's previous lives.
62. Vaipulya — comprises nine important Mahāyāna sūtras; 'Aśtasahsrikā prajñā paramita, 'Saddharma pundrīka', 'Lalita-vistara', 'Lankāvatara'; 'Suvarṇa-prabhāṣa', 'Ganda-vyuha', 'Tathāgata-guhyaka', 'Samādhirāja' and 'Daśa-bhumiśvara', these are called 'Vaipulya-sutraś owing to their comprehensiveness ('vipulatā').
63. adbhuta dharma — one of the nine 'angas' of dharma literature; contains descriptions of the miracles and mysteries of Tathāgata.
64. upadeśa-varga — comprises the Lord's discourses.
65. kāya-prasrabdhi — bodily peace.
66. vyāseka — diversion, disturbance.
67. pudgala dharmas — individual tendencies.
68. pancha-skandha — 'skandha' means a heap, a group or 'samudāya'; the five mental tendencies: 'rūpa' (form comprising physical tendencies), 'vedanā' (feeling), 'samjñā' (cognition), 'samskāra' (collection of mental aggregates) and 'vijñāna'(knowledge of external things and internal tendencies).
69. dvādaśāyatanas — 'ayatana' is defined as 'ayama tanoti itī' 'āyatana', 'ayama' means 'praveśama' or entrance, the twelve (dvādaśa) entrances (āyatanas) are the six senses and six sense objects; eye, ear, nose, tongue, touch, intellect and form, sound, smell, taste, touch, dharmas (not within the ambit of external senses).
70. aṣṭādaśa dhātu — six sense objects, six senses and six cognitions.
71. chitta-vipathanā svabhāva — the nature of appearances in the mind.
72. sāsrava — those which produce unclean 'dharmas'.
73. anāsrava — clean.
74. vedanā — feeling.

75. samjña — consciousness, cognition.
76. samskāra — mental aggregates.
77. vijñāna — special cognition.
78. parihāra — relinquishment, giving up.
79. kalpanā — imagination, fictional mind.
80. araṇi — tinder stick for producing fire.
81. animitta yoga — 'dhyāna' leads to 'vimokśa' and 'vimokśa' leads to yoga; in each stage one power is attained; the first stage is 'śunyatā' and the second is 'animitta'.
82. nirnimittatā — the awareness of the emptiness of phenomena.
83. apratiṣthata dhyāna — disturbed meditation, without fixation on 'rūpa' and 'samsāra'.
84. anupalambha dhyāna — non-perceptive meditation.
85. prachāra — menifestation, instigation.
86. anabhisamskāra-vāhitā — an approach of natural ease.
87. bhoga — taste, enjoyment.
88. ābhoga — effort.
89. prahara — lit. 'stroke', division of time, about one eighth part of a day.
90. ārya-bhadracharyā — the routine conduct of a noble being.
91. anapagati — non-falling down, non-deviation, non-deflection.
92. paripāka — maturation.
93. Kaśirāja probably refers to the story of 'śivi' the king of Vārāṇasi whose adherance to compassion was put to severe test by the devas. Indra, disguised as a falcon, pounced upon its victim, a pigeon. As the king tried to rescue the bird, the falcon said, "you are depriving me of my right, I have a claim on my shikār." The just and compassionate king offered his own flesh if the falcon let off the pigeon. The falcon agreed but the helpless bird grew heavier in the scales as king Śivi went on slicing flesh from his own body to equal the weight of the pigeon. Pleased with such sense of compassion Indra appeared in his true form, blessed the king and restored him back to health as before.
94. kuśala mūlas — meritorious roots of actions as give good results.
95. tīrthikas — brahmin scholars who did not subscribe to Buddha's gospel; some of the famous tīrthika teachers contemporaneous with Buddha were; Poorna-kaśyapa, Maskari Goshāli-putra, Sanjayi vairathi-putra, Ajit keśa-kambala, Kakuda-kātyāyana, Nirgrantha-jñātiputra.
96. prayoga — exercise, experiment.
97. priṣtalabdha — past achievement, inherited, previously accumulated.
98. apoṣa — non-performance, non-stability.

99. a-pudgala — non-being, non-self existence of beings.
100. āśaya-nirvāṇa — aimed release as in Hinayāna; 'āśaya' is objective; nirvāṇa as an objective.
101. riddhi — powers of special attainment.
102. daśa-bhumiśvara — one of the most well known 'vaipulya sutras' which was first translated into Chinese in 297 A.D. by Dharmarakśa.
103. kārya-nispatti — completeness, proficiency in work.
104. priṣtalabdha — later attainment.
105. vyavadāna — cleansing, 'viśuddhatā'.

GLOSSARY - III

1. aparimita — limitless.
2. apramāṇa — also termed 'apramāṇya', because countless 'jivas' (creatures) are the 'ālambana' of this 'samādhi', which comprises 'maitri' (love), 'karuṇā' (compassion), 'muditā' (joy) and 'upekśā' (detachment), the four 'brahma-viharas'; the term 'apramāṇa' is used in 'ārya-dharma' scriptures.
3. dauṣthula — wickedness.
4. nimitta — an object, an aim, its motive cause.
5. nirvilkalpa pratibimbakama — a reflection, which is the result of direct perception.
6. savikalpa pratibimbakama — a reflection, which is the result of mental acquisition.
7. vastu-paryantatā — the ultimate of things.
8. kārya-pariniṣpatti — fulfilment of work or objective.
9. avikalpa — without alternatives, undifferentiated.
10. tattva-nirupaṅa vikalpa — analytical option.
11. vastu-paryantatva — the limits of phenomena.
12. paryanta — limit, end, boundary.
13. rasāyana — elixir.
14. āśraya-pravritti — attainable through the path of transcendental or undifferentiated 'jñāna', 'buddhattva'.
15. kārya samāpatti — absorption in work.
16. śruta — that which is heard from an instructor or a teacher's lips.
17. chintana — reflection, contemplation. 'śruta-maya' 'chitana-maya' and 'bhāvanā-maya' are practising ('prayogika') dharmas.
18. anuvyanjanā — artistry, expression.
19. parsana-maṇḍala — boddhisattvas, jinas — the family ('parivāra') of Buddha; his entourage.
20. rūpi-arūpa-bheda — the world is made up of names and forms ('name — rupātmaka'); both are related to skandhas; the difference of 'form' and 'non-form' — rūpi (with form) and 'arūpa' (without form).
21. rūpa-skandha — form heaps.
22. vedanā-skandha — feeling heaps.
23. apratibhāsa — non-reflection.
24. vastu-sata — the ultimate or 'paramartha' of things; it is 'nirvikalpa'.
25. bhāva-'is-ness' — feeling thereof, they are 'śunya' in essence'
26. prapanch — falsehood, illusion.
27. nirnimitta yoga — undifferentiated yoga.
28. vyāpaka — pervasive.
29. vyāpya — object of pervasiveness.

30. kausidya — laziness, lethargy, opposite of valour ('veerya').
31. sampramoṣa — forsaking.
32. laya — lethargic absorption of mind.
33. audhatya — insolence of mind.
34. anābhoga — non-effort.
35. ābhoga — effort.
36. aṣta-prahāṇa samskāra — eight 'samskāras' that help removal of faults.
37. śraddhā — mental bliss, faith.
38. chhanda — desire to work ('kartu-kāmyatā').
39. vyāyāma — exercise; exposition.
40. prasrabdhi — calmness; peace, activeness of body; opposite of 'dauṣthulya'.
41. smriti — recollectedness.
42. samprajñāya — awareness.
43. chetanā — that consciousness which understands 'samyaka hetu' and 'mithyā hetu' characteristics.
44. anusmriti — *lit.* 'to remember again and again or 'anurūpa smriti', i.e. proper rememberance of that which is of benefit to the yogi in his 'sādhanā'; the ten kinds of the objects of 'anusmriti' are; 'buddhānusmriti', 'dharmānusmriti', 'samghānusmriti', 'śitānusmriti', 'lābhānusmriti', 'devatān-nusmriti', 'kāyāgatātma-smriti', 'maraṇānusmriti', 'anāpānanusmriti', 'upaśamanānusmriti'.
45. chitta-nirodha — cessation of the mind.
46. chaturtha-dhyāna — the last of the four 'dhyānas' or 'dhyāna-chatuṣṭaka' specified for a yogi, it has two parts; 'upekśā-vedanā' and 'ekāgratā' — feeling of detachment and concentration, all 'vitarka' (contradictions) disappear and 'detachment becomes totally refined during this meditation.
47. asattvas — non-true existence of beings.
48. Dārikā — daughter.
49. bahūśruti — scholarly, erudite.
50. ayoniśa — perversion (of belief); wrong dharmas.
51. ājivakavāda — belief in destiny and that both the learned and the ignorant lead their destined lives and moving through cyclic existence and their 'dukha'; it believes neither in karma nor its fruit, founded by Makkali Gosal, one of the six famous teachers who were contemporaries of Buddha; Makkali lived in a hut behind 'Jetavana'.
52. kśetra-pariśuddhi — purification, sanctifying a (Buddha) - field, (buddhatva' is attained through 'punya' and 'jñāna' accumulations; Buddhas, who do not enter 'śunyatā' after fulfilling their vow of service to 'sattvas' earn a field ('kśetra') for

themselves which is sacred and sanctified with divine attributes).

53. prabhā — the gloss of divinity, aura.
54. parivāra — the Buddha-family of boddhisattvas, 'jinas' divine beings and deities who surround Buddha or live in their own different spheres like 'sukhāvati'.
55. mahābhoga — having a large compass, great enjoyment, providing others with it.
56. pratimokśa samvara — the vow for the deliverance of 'sattvas' from 'samsāra'.
57. aupalambhika — one who makes available, a donor, a giver.
58. prāmrista — violated, afflicted with disease.
59. dāna-pariyesthitā — lapses in giving.
60. parikalpita — imagined, fictionalised with 'hetu' (cause) and 'pratyaya' (casual factor).
61. niṣparikalpa — without 'hetu' and 'pratyaya' absolute.
62. vyākaraṇa — 'vyākhya', exposition, explanation.
63. Dipankara — a bodhisattva.
64. animitta-vihara-pāramatā — capacity to roam in 'animitta'.
65. avaivartika — not-returning.
66. mridu indriya — soft senses, gentle.
67. tikśaṇa indriya — sharp senses.
68. samudāchāra — appearance, manifestation.
69. pariśiṣta — appendix, residual; also name of a class of works supplementing sutras.
70. tyāga — renunciation.
71. mahātyāga — great renunciation.
72. ati-tyāga — total renunciation.
73. gomaya-maṇḍala — 'maṇḍala' made of 'gomaya' or cow-dung.
74. maṇḍala — circular disc, orb.
75. nirodha samāpatti — the absorption state when there is cessation of all dharmas.
76. viśuddhatartama kśaṇa — 'kśaṇa' or 'viśeṣa' is the experience of 'paramārtha dravya' (the ultimate substance) which is 'arūpi' (formless); while 'jñāna', Dinnaga speaks of as 'pratyakśa' (manifest) and 'anumana' (guess) as its two prongs, because a subject is either 'viśeṣa' (special) or 'sāmānya' (ordinary); 'viśeṣa' is the equivalent of 'kśaṇa', because it is that which is realised through 'vivechanā' (analysis) and is free from all 'sāmānya' (ordinary) characteristics.
77. dharma-dhātu — the true essence of things, the equivalent of 'tathatā', 'śunyatā', 'bhūta-koti'.